# The Children's Nurse

# The
# Children's Nurse

*The True Story of a*
*Great Ormond Street Nurse*

## Susan Macqueen
with Georgina Rodgers

This edition first published in Great Britain in 2013 by
Orion Books
an imprint of the Orion Publishing Group Ltd
Orion House, 5 Upper St Martin's Lane,
London WC2H 9EA
An Hachette UK Company

1 3 5 7 9 10 8 6 4 2

A CIP catalogue record for this book is
available from the British Library.

ISBN: 9781 4091 2916 5

Typeset by Input Data Services Ltd, Bridgwater, Somerset

Printed and bound by CPI Group (UK) Ltd, Croydon, CR0 4YY

The Orion Publishing Group's policy is to use papers
that are natural, renewable and recyclable and made
from wood grown in sustainable forests. The logging
and manufacturing processes are expected to conform to
the environmental regulations of the country of origin.

Every effort has been made to fulfil requirements
with regard to reproducing copyright material.
The author and publisher will be glad to rectify any
omissions at the earliest opportunity.

*I dedicate this book to all the talented paediatric nurses and doctors, past and present, who helped make my career so fruitful and to the children and their parents who made it all worthwhile.*

*And to my husband, John, for his continual support and good humour.*

# Acknowledgements

I wish to thank the following people for their guidance in producing this book:

Liz Morgan, Chief Nurse at GOSH, for her encouragement and support. The Executive Committee of the GOSH Nurse's League who have supported me unfailingly as their President. My Editor Jane Sturrock, Nicki Crossley and the team at Orion for all their work and having faith in the project. Rowan Lawton, my agent, who introduced me to the concept and guided me through the process. Finally, but by no means least, my wonderful ghostwriter Georgina Rodgers, for approaching me with the idea for the book in the first place and for all her hard work, patience and efforts in bringing my story to life.

# Contents

'Nurses are our best helpers; if indeed it be not rather true and I feel it is true, they are the real carriers-on of the hospital ... They indeed are those who lead while we tread in their steps, and that often humbly and at a long distance.'

DR CHARLES WEST,
*Founder of Great Ormond Street Hospital*
(1816–98)

# I

# First Impressions

As I walked up Great Ormond Street, the façade of the famous hospital stood before me, grand and awesome, freckled with shadows. The morning was a typically autumnal British one – grey, damp and cold, with ominous rain clouds scuttling across the sky and crispy leaves dancing in the wind like burnt orange-and-yellow waves. It was 1969, the year Neil Armstrong became the first man to set foot on the moon. I was twenty-four years old, eager and excited about the new chapter in my nursing career.

I had walked the short journey from my spartan room in the nurses' home in Guilford Street to which I had moved the previous weekend. It was linked to the hospital via a bridge corridor but I needed some fresh air and thought a brisk walk might help to calm my frayed nerves. Despite the early hour, luminous blue sirens blared past, causing me to slam my hands against my numb ears. There was no such luxury as double glazing in my new home; it was a fairly new concept back then so I was chilled to the bone before I set out. We were at the back of Great Ormond Street Children's Hospital, surrounded by the Institute of Child Health, University College Hospital, the National Hospital for Nervous Diseases, the Italian Hospital and the Homeopathic Hospital. I would soon learn that the ear-splitting wailing from the sirens would be the soundtrack to my time there.

I pulled my red-lined, navy wool cape tighter around myself as I deftly skirted the muddy puddles, so that my regulation black shoes and thick nylon tights would remain as clean as possible. It wouldn't do to turn up on my first day covered in muck.

As I walked through the grand courtyard of the historic Southwood Building I looked up at the weather-worn, gunmetal-coloured high-rise block. Each ward on the seven floors had a small balcony so that the children could venture outside, but for safety it was covered with a metal grille which made the building look forbidding, like some sort of prison. The air was thick with dark, grey fog and heavy with petrol fumes. Everyone smoked in those days, indoors as well as out. It was even allowed in hospitals for a long time, which seems crazy now. My mother, Violet, smoked all her life. When I had first started nursing a few years previously and it was seen as the height of sophistication, I had taken up the habit too, but stopped smoking after a few years.

I later learnt that entertainment for the children was common at the hospital's outside entrance. Enormous police horses, steam rising from their backs, would come and the children would pat their warm muzzles and laugh as the horses snorted. On other occasions, a fire engine would stop at the entrance and the children would be helped up the steps into the front seat. They would sit on the knee of one of the friendly firemen, yellow helmets falling over their eyes, and pretend to drive the vehicle. Those who could not leave the wards would either walk on to the balcony to watch, or their beds would be wheeled outside and they would be propped up so they could see the fun below. One year a circus even came into the hospital courtyard, with glowing roundabouts, stalls where the children could hook bright yellow ducks out of a paddling pool to win prizes, jugglers on stilts and clowns with wide, red smiles. It was such a hit, I don't know who enjoyed it more – the adults or the children.

At the hospital's narrow, glass revolving doors, people were rushing in and out, including staff, parents, and children. Some of the children were clutching their parents' hands; others were being pushed in wheelchairs or helped from ambulances, which at that time resembled large, round buses. A small child on a trolley was being wheeled from the front of the hospital to the side entrance on the right, which led to Admissions, where they would be seen by a doctor and taken straight to one of the wards.

Once inside, a red leather-covered bench sat along one wall; above it was a large painting of a gentle-looking, buxom nurse dressed in a grey uniform with long sleeves and a frilly lace hat: a matron from the distant past.

'Mornin', Nurse,' one of the porters greeted me with a toothy smile, from behind a wooden desk. His voice had a distinct East End ring to it. He was smartly dressed in a navy jumper, blue shirt and trousers.

'Hello,' I said, my heart still beating fast, both from my walk and first-day nerves.

'I've not seen that face before. You're new 'ere?' he asked.

'I am,' I replied. 'First day.'

'Ahh, thought so. I'm Tom, the head porter. Nothing is too much trouble, so if you need parcels taking to the Post Office, or extra beds or oxygen cylinders, you know where to find me.'

'Thank you,' I replied. Tom had broken the ice and

I started to feel calmer and welcomed into this small, tightly woven community.

As I looked around I felt a fire in my belly.

At that point in my career, after three years' training at Addenbrooke's Hospital in Cambridge, I was known as a 'GT', a General Trained Nurse. I had also done some midwifery training in Bristol and spent two years as a staff nurse on the paediatric ward at Addenbrooke's. It took thirteen months to qualify as a paediatric nurse at GOSH and until then I would be known as a 'string'. As I headed towards my first assignment, I felt quietly confident that I might have a small head start at Great Ormond Street compared with my fellow 'strings'. I thought I had experienced quite a lot already during my nursing training and role as a staff nurse: surely I would be okay?

The small changing room in the cardiac ward smelt sweet – of sweat and disinfectant – and was messy, with shoes and items of clothing strewn all over the place, like a jumble sale. It was in stark contrast to the order of the ward I was about to enter. There were no proper lockers at the time so I would have to leave my handbag in the sister's office.

As I peeled off my heavy cloak, I felt glad of the warmth of the hospital. Underneath was my new pink-and-white striped short-sleeved uniform. I was skinny as a rake back then, with long, Bambi-like legs, and had short mousy-brown hair and thick glasses. On my head I wore a 'string's cap' – a white, starched cap with a smart goffered rim and fan-shaped top – into which I tucked the fine wisps of my hair and secured it with white hair-grips. The look was completed with my white apron,

4

which was starched rigid. A simple silver pocket watch hung from my pinafore. I was now officially a 'pink nurse', as they were known in other hospitals. Pink nurses who went on to complete their adult training elsewhere would always wear their GOSH uniforms, marking them apart from everyone else.

I smoothed down my apron and inhaled deeply. I wanted to make the best possible impression and knew the senior staff on my first ward would be taking notes on my appearance. The pink nurses were renowned for their attention to detail, not only in the way they looked, but in the way they behaved and cared for their patients. They always dried between the tiny toes of their charges, put toothpaste on the children's toothbrushes for them and helped them comb their hair before bed. I hoped that I would live up to the hospital's high standards.

I headed into the cardiac ward with my nerves in shreds; my palms felt clammy and I could feel my heart beating in my chest like a drum. As I listened to the handover – a time-honoured tradition where the incoming shift of nurses would receive a report on every patient's care to provide continuity – in the Sister's office, there were references to diseases and abnormalities I had never heard of. Everything was abbreviated and I was confused. The doctors and other more senior nurses talked quickly and without pause, as if they were speaking a foreign language. The ward had several sisters, as one had to be on duty twenty-four hours a day, along with a team of senior staff nurses, staff nurses and students doing their cardiac training. It was very busy and everyone but me seemed to know everything. I felt completely out of my depth.

My first impression of the seventeen-bedded L-shaped ward was that it was very noisy and extremely cramped. Because there were so many people and so much equipment everywhere I turned, it seemed like an intensive care unit. A friendly young woman by the name of Staff Nurse Peacock was the first person I was introduced to. She was a tall girl with hair the colour of the autumn leaves scattered outside on the pavement. She greeted me with a friendly, lopsided grin and a firm handshake and told me she had been working in the cardiac ward for several months. I eagerly accepted her offer to show me round and followed her as she strode off, pointing things out as we went.

Many of the children were on ventilators, machines that supported their breathing. At that time these were called Engstroms; they were big, green with black rubber tubing, and made a rhythmic, whooshing noise. Some of the children on ventilators were sitting up playing with toys, painting or drawing pictures and laughing. I had only been used to children and adults on ventilators being unconscious or lying in bed seriously ill, so I felt quite shocked by this, but tried not to show it. My family and friends say I never give anything away in my facial expression.

'The long-term ventilated children become so used to the noise in a comforting way, we often have to wean them off it, or else they panic. We'll just leave them on in the corner,' the sister said.

'How long for?' I asked.

'Usually about thirty-six to forty-eight hours but it depends on the child, of course. We try to take them on short walks so they get used to other noises on the ward.'

As well as patients, there were parents, siblings, nurses and doctors gathered around bedsides and one child sat reading his times tables aloud to a lady who was obviously a schoolteacher. There were machines clicking, cardiac monitors beeping and the constant hum of people talking, children laughing, shrieking, crying and playing. The ward smelt of chemicals, but although some of the fabric on the seats was old and worn, it looked clean. Most of the children, like those at Addenbrooke's, were dressed and wearing their own clothes, unlike adult hospital patients who usually wore pyjamas or hospital gowns.

Getting the children up and ready for the day each morning was one of the first things we did in paediatric wards. It brought a sense of normality to the department.

'Do they bring their own clothes?' I asked.

'Yes, and there are loads of donations,' Staff Nurse Peacock told me. 'There's also a knitting room on one of the lower floors of the hospital, where a group of volunteers come every week to knit and crochet clothes for the children. If Sister asks, they'll whip up whatever we want if we give them the size and colour. The knitters are lovely people and the clothes are wonderful. The sisters even take them home to wash so they don't get ruined in the hospital laundry.'

Just before the entrance to the ward, there was a basic waiting room, which looked out on to the back of the nurses' home. The only contents were a small red sofa, a mirror and some cupboards that were packed to the brim, with what looked like old Christmas decorations poking out of them. Next door was a room where all the trays and equipment were put into a huge metal tank, to be boiled and sterilised. As we went in, my glasses steamed up and my hat started to wilt.

Staff Nurse Peacock looked over and laughed; she too wore spectacles.

'Annoying, isn't it?' she said with a chuckle, before moving on to show me the next room: Sister's office.

'This is where there are the best treats,' she said, pointing to an open box of Roses chocolates, which sat alongside some wilting flowers in a vase. 'The parents are very kind and are always giving us presents,' she said. My stomach grumbled; I had struggled to eat breakfast that morning.

Finally, there was the treatment room where all the sterile equipment and drugs were stored. Despite its name, no children had their treatment in there; it was always given on the ward. This room was piled high with disposable equipment, such as ventilator tubing, connections, all the intravenous equipment and bags of fluid, urinary bags, oxygen tubes and masks, dressings and bandages, temperature probes, cotton wool, gauze, syringes and needles.

'Ordering new stock is an important job,' Staff Nurse Peacock told me. 'If you forget, you are in the doghouse. Stock is topped up by the "runner" who arranges the delivery of equipment when it is needed and keeps the show on the road. You will get a go at being the runner during your time with us.'

I secretly hoped that moment would still be some time away; there seemed to be so much to remember.

Then we went down a short corridor and, to the left, there was a three-bedded cubicle, which held children who were mostly recovering from operations. The nurses' station was outside a six-bedded bay containing children of less than a year, the majority of them on ventilators, and this was where I was to start my training. Turning right into another corridor around the L-shaped ward, there were several single cubicles on both sides.

All the bed areas displayed paintings of animals or classic Hans Christian Andersen fairy tales, some obviously drawn by the play leader and some by the children who were good at art. All the curtains were of different patterns because they were sent off to the laundry at different times. Most of the children also had pictures they had drawn stuck to the wall behind their beds, like an enormous fridge door. It was a riot of colour and decoration; a world away from the gloomy and drab surroundings I had experienced on adult wards during my training.

There was an emergency red light outside each bed area, which lit up if someone pressed the buzzer to indicate which child required emergency care.

Three bed spaces in two cubicles knocked into one at the end of the corridor served as the 'post pump' area; these were for children who had undergone open-heart surgery.

'These patients have two nurses to look after them for twenty-four to forty-eight hours, or longer if there are complications,' the staff nurse continued. 'There are sometimes cardiac arrests here. It's always quite tense so we only put the most senior nurses with post-pump children. It can be quite hard.'

The idea of working in this area filled me with dread. I would never cope or know what to do, I thought. It seemed filled with mystery and drama and the fine line that I knew hovered between life and death.

'You'll be trained to nurse these patients and how to deal with complications. Arrests and bleeding are very common,' she went on. 'You'll need to look after at least one of these patients under supervision during your time here.'

I felt like burying my head in the sand and hoping it would never happen. I had heard a rumour at the nurses' home that if you weren't very competent, you would never be put here at all.

At the end of the ward was another cubicle being used to disinfect the ventilator tubing, and just beyond that a space where all the ventilators were stored. A ventilator technician was responsible for ensuring that they were cleaned and in working order and that there were enough machines for the following day's operations and any emergency admissions. Staff Nurse Peacock also showed me where the resuscitation trolley was – I hoped I would never have to use it – and where baby feeds were kept in the fridge. There seemed so many feeds: some were expressed breast milk, others SMA formula, and others still were special diet feeds. The drugs trolley carried an array of drugs that I knew would be given out in tiny doses according to the patient's body weight. I felt horribly overwhelmed; I had so much to learn and felt as if I would never get to grips with so much new information.

The six-bedded area to which I was assigned, where the children under twelve months were nursed, was apparently the 'easy' area. The majority of them were on ventilators following heart operations and most had their own nurse, known as a 'special'.

The first child I was to look after was Henry, an eight-month-old who had an atrial septal defect (ASD), a hole in the heart. He was going for open-heart surgery that morning. Even though I knew I could go to a more senior nurse with questions and worries, I was so nervous that my mouth kept going dry and my teeth stuck to my lips. I needed a drink of water but was just too busy to attend to my own needs. Not only was Henry my first patient at GOSH, but he was also the first child I had ever looked after who had had this type of surgery.

After giving him his pre-med, a combination of drugs which was given to him prior his anaesthetic to help sedate him at 9 a.m., the head porter appeared to collect Henry and I saw that he made the other children laugh by pulling silly faces and plucking pennies from behind his ears. I accompanied them both to theatre where I watched Henry being anaesthetised before handing him over to the theatre nurses. Parents weren't allowed into the anaesthetic room at that time. Henry's mum, Carol, a pretty and fashionable young lady in her twenties, and her husband, Graham, who must have been ten years older and looked rather remote, were anxiously waiting on the ward. Carol had her brown hair in a sleek bob, backcombed into a bouffant at the top, and a thick fur jacket rested on her shoulders. As I went to speak to her I noticed that despite being immaculately made-up with heavy eyeliner, her eyes were glassy with tears.

'Is Henry okay?' She jumped up as soon as she saw me.

'He's fine. He went into theatre five minutes ago. He'll be about four hours. Maybe it would be easier if you went out and had a break?'

I knew that this was a good opportunity for parents to go out. Somehow, leaving the ward during surgery was easier for them than sitting in the waiting room, where the minutes would tick by agonisingly slowly as they looked anxiously at the clock. Sometimes, if the parents had been staying at the hospital for a while, we would even suggest that it was a good time to do their washing. There weren't any washing machines in the hospital then so they would go to the launderette around the corner in Lamb's Conduit Street and pass the time surrounded by steam. Others might decide to go to Oxford Street and, in a daze, wander round one of the busy department stores, like John Lewis or Marshall & Snelgrove.

'Come on, Carol. Let's go and get a cup of tea.' Graham stood up, pulling himself to his full height of six foot plus, put a solid, suited arm around his wife and led her away. He was extremely well spoken and I would soon learn that the hospital at that time was quite elitist and mainly the domain of affluent, white, middle-class offspring, although of course there were always exceptions for seriously ill children.

I then returned to the ward to systematically prepare Henry's bed area, putting clean sheets on the bed and ensuring that the suction and oxygen were working. There was a huge amount of equipment to make ready to see me through the shift, including an intravenous stand for hanging the IV bags, chest-drain clamps, tracheostomy dilators, which we called 'trachy' dilators – the piece of equipment used to insert the tracheostomy – a spare trachy tube in case the tube became misplaced, clean suction trays, the correct medical charts and other essential items. I checked that the ventilator technician was bringing a ventilator and that there were enough electrodes for the cardiac monitor. I knew I had to be methodical and organised because the pressure would be on as soon as Henry got back from theatre. I noted where the resuscitation trolley was and made sure that it been checked in case of an emergency, even though I knew that it was examined daily and each time it was used. I prayed that I wouldn't have to use it on this occasion.

As I worked my way through the tasks I had to complete before I even set eyes on my post-operative patient, I started to settle into a steady rhythm but still felt tense. I knew that I needed to prove myself more than ever now that I was finally at GOSH. It was important to be aware if anything was going wrong while I worked: Would I remember to chart everything? Would Henry be okay? Would there be complications? What if I missed something? Questions rattled through my head and I felt overwrought.

When the call came that the operation was over, I was helping one of my colleagues to give an injection to another child, so Staff Nurse Peacock collected Henry for me and brought him back to the ward. Carol and Graham had returned by then; the doctor had told them that the operation had gone well but, understandably, they were eager to see their little boy.

I later learnt that most parents would hold your estimate of the time the procedure would take to the minute, and if the child was still in theatre when they came back, they would panic. For this reason we always made sure that someone was around to tell them what was going on.

'Come and see him briefly,' I said to Henry's parents. 'And then if you sit in the waiting room while we settle him, I'll call you again when we're ready for you.'

I wanted to appear confident in front of them, so as to reassure them that I could look after their little boy. However, there were certain things I was unsure about, like charting ventilator readings and how to milk Henry's chest drains, so I quickly sought out Staff Nurse Peacock to question her about them.

When Henry arrived back on the ward he looked tiny and was covered in tubes; I could barely see him in the cot. I felt an overwhelming urge to do the best job I possibly could for him and his parents.

Carol and Graham were both wide-eyed with shock. However thoroughly parents prepare themselves for seeing their baby after an operation, I think it is always hugely upsetting. They stroked his tiny hands with tears in their eyes. They seemed unaware of their surroundings and just focused on their child, praying he would be okay.

'Come on then, let's get you settled,' I said to Henry, as I took over and they went outside and waited.

My to-do list was as follows: I had to take Henry's pulse every quarter of an hour; his temperature every hour; his blood pressure every half-hour; take quarter-hourly readings on the ventilator; do mouth care every hour; milk the two chest drains to remove excess fluid every half-hour and measure the amounts drained. He also had an endo-tracheal inserted in, a tube that is passed into the windpipe via the nose and connected to an oxygen supply, and a ventilator to assist with breathing, which I would need to suction every quarter of an hour. Many of the other children had tracheostomies to provide longer-term ventilation. There were intra-venous infusions, drips, which needed recording every half-hour. I also had to check whether Henry passed any urine and the wound and chest drains had to be checked for bleeding. His naso-gastric tube needed aspiration every hour. On top of all this, I had to check any drugs he was due and every procedure had to be charted.

I felt as if I didn't have time to think whether what I was doing was right; I was just trying to get everything done. I religiously kept doing all the observations, often with Carol and Graham looking on. If I was in the middle of something and they asked me a question, I got a few minutes behind and started to fret. It felt like a marathon and beads of sweat trickled down my back as I worked.

I also had to change Henry's nappy regularly. There was a great ritual over nappy-changing at GOSH; nappies were called 'sundries'. During the day, each baby would be dressed and put on to a draw sheet, a small sheet over the top of the bed, with a red rubber mat underneath. A smaller red rubber mat would be placed under the baby's bottom, with a square muslin nappy on top. The baby would have the muslin nappy next to the skin and a terry-towelling nappy on the outside. I don't know how many nappies we got through during a day – a mountain for sure – because the children were changed four-hourly, or as necessary. The used nappies were put into a bucket and soaked in disinfectant, sluiced, and then sent off to the laundry. It seems crazy these days to think about life before disposable nappies because dealing with the 'sundries' was a job in itself.

Somehow I made it through the shift and at 3 p.m. I handed over to another nurse so that I could go for a late lunch in the canteen. Henry looked clean, tidy and comfortable and I felt a mixture of things, mainly exhaustion, but also overwhelming relief, and satisfaction that I had achieved something. I was thankful to escape from the ward for a break.

It would take me a while to get orientated within the hospital. I didn't have time to explore the many wards as I was too busy looking after Henry and the short lunch break didn't help. The building felt like a maze, despite the fact that most wards were built in the same L-shape. This was so that one side could be closed down if there was an outbreak of infection.

The canteen occupied a room on the ground floor of the nurses' home, so I went down the stone stairs and back along the bridge corridor I had crossed earlier in the day. The sisters had a separate dining room opposite, which the likes of us students were never allowed to enter. Our canteen was a large, slightly dingy room with high ceilings and magnolia paint peeling from the walls. The serving hatches sat at one end and the smell of food hung in the air, but at least it was free, which was a huge bonus for us because we were always short of money. There was not much focus on healthy eating in those days because people were generally more active, and on my first day I chose what looked like a meat stew with potatoes and vegetables, followed by spotted dick and custard. The custard had a thick, jelly-like skin on top of it. I sat eating my tepid meal in quite a daze and was happy not to have to talk to anyone.

When I took over Henry again after lunch I settled into the routine more quickly, but still felt overwhelmed at times, especially if someone interrupted me. By then, Graham had gone home to look after Henry's sister and Carol told me how difficult he found the fact that his son was ill.

'I think he thinks he's to blame somehow,' she said. 'I tell him that it's ridiculous but he hates talking about it and is so hard to read. I never know how he's feeling. I worry about him almost as much as I do about Henry. I know Henry's in good hands here and will be fine.'

'Men, eh? They find it hard to talk about things – they

bottle it up more,' I replied. I often found that this was the case, especially with parents who came from well-to-do families. Women, on the other hand, talked about everything and sharing their fears and thoughts always made it easier for them to cope.

We arranged for Carol to spend the night on a Z-Bed in the waiting room and it was clearly a far cry from the comfort of her home. When I saw her at the end of my shift, gone was her beehive hairstyle and pristine eye-liner, but she was clearly happier and calmer now that the day had gone smoothly.

Before leaving, I checked if she needed anything, such as a towel, and made sure she knew where she could take a shower.

'How do you think Henry is doing?' I asked.

'Better,' she replied. One thing I would have drummed into me time and time again throughout my career was how important it was to listen to the mother; they knew their child better than anyone: their routines, temperament, the pitch of their cry. There is an intrinsic connection between mother and child.

'Have the doctors said anything else?' I asked.

'No, but they did say they would see Henry first thing in the morning when they do their rounds. I know he's comfortable.'

'That's good. I'll see you in the morning too. Good night.'

'Good night, Nurse,' she replied. 'And thank you.'

As I left the hospital, I was still buzzing with the adrenalin of the day and decided to go for a walk to familiarise myself with my surroundings. I headed up Southampton Row, passing busy pubs and men in pinstriped suits clutching brown leather briefcases, dashing for the tube.

When I was nearly at King's Cross, I decided it was time to head back to the nurses' home. Walking down a dark and sooty street, I could only hear the clip of my shoes on the pavement until, suddenly, a screechy voice piped up from the darkness.

'This is my patch – get lost, love! Get out!'

I looked towards the voice and staring back at me was a middle-aged lady dressed in old fishnet tights, plastic-looking short pants, spiky high heels, and with a leather jacket hanging off her bony shoulders. Her bosoms jutted rudely out of her gaunt, pale chest. She had skin as wrinkled as yesterday's newspaper and she appeared to be sneering at me. A cigarette was hanging loosely from her bright red lips, the end glowing like a yellow beacon in the inky dark.

The reality hit me: the woman was a prostitute. It was a bit of a bolt from the blue and left me slightly stunned and rooted to the spot. But I quickly shifted my gaze, put my head down and scurried as fast as I could back to the nurses' home. I now knew which areas to avoid at night. It seemed as if everything in London changed under the cover of darkness, unlike Cambridge, which was very sedate in comparison.

'Ha, ha, you get yourself home, darlin',' the woman shouted after me.

This was not like the world I had been used to. I felt a little scared; I'd heard so many stories about this huge, sprawling city and here I was, naïve and innocent and not at all sure what to expect.

I was to learn more about the reality of these women's lives when I found myself dealing with patients with HIV and AIDS. They were often abused, beaten, suffered from sexually transmitted diseases or were hooked on Class A drugs supplied by their pimp. No woman deserves to be so desperate that she is forced on to the streets. The raw image of this woman still remains in my mind.

However, I soon calmed down and started to feel excited about being in London. There were endless opportunities on the social front, such as the many lively theatres, galleries and buzzing pubs, right on my doorstep. If I wanted to, I could visit a new venue nearly every day of my thirteen months. But I knew I shouldn't get carried away; if my first day at GOSH was anything to go by, I knew I would need to study hard to get through my training and would often be exhausted. The sights, sounds and thrills of London would have to be enjoyed on my days off only.

When some of the other nurses in my group, or 'set' as it was known then, came off duty, we all met in the canteen for dinner. All of us had animated stories to tell about our day's work and when I recounted what I had been through, there was obvious interest.

'Gosh, you must've been terrified.' ... 'Talk about jumping in at the deep end.' ... 'I don't know how I would've survived,' they all chimed, as we tucked into a bland chicken dish followed by treacle sponge.

Now that my first day was over, I was feeling pretty good about myself, having coped reasonably well, but I couldn't help feeling that I had drawn the short straw. Some of the others had not been allowed to do much by the staff nurses who were mentoring them, and had spent their time feeding or bathing babies.

After supper, we went into the cosy sitting room and flopped in the comfy armchairs, chatting over coffee. This nurses' lounge was opened in 1934. Today the last-remaining feature is the fine ornamental fireplace, which we used to huddle around. We were all feeling tired, but relieved that we had made it that far, and decided that an early night was in order as we would be up at the crack of dawn the following day.

Just before I went to bed, I rang home on a payphone to tell my mother about the first day and to let her know I was okay. I knew she would be worrying about me.

'Oh Sue, I'm so glad you called,' she said, as soon as she heard my voice. 'I've been thinking about you all day.'

'I'm fine, Mum. Today was challenging, but it went really well.' I gave her a brief overview of what I had been doing and promised that I would ring again soon.

'Really?' she teased.

I often didn't ring home when I should and was always being told off about it. I would tell my mother that no news was good news, but she never believed me.

'You and your brother are as bad as each other,' she would say.

My brother Peter, who is nine years younger than me, was just as slack about calling home. We were even worse when it came to phoning each other. We were both so wrapped up in our separate lives that often several months would pass before I would talk to Peter. Instead, we used to relay family information to one another through my mother. At least Mum knew what we were both up to.

The next day, I was not sure who I would be looking after, so again I felt anxious as I approached the hospital, especially as I now had a flavour of what was to come. Luckily it was Henry. Although still tense, I gradually started to relax and gain confidence but each time I looked after a child, the feeling came back.

As the days wore on, I got to know Graham and Carol better. I realised that the ward sister would always try and keep the same nurses for each patient, if possible. This was because the family and the child would feel more secure with a familiar, smiling face around, and the nurse would feel that she was caring for the whole child, not just treating their illness but getting to know their likes and dislikes. This was very important to young children, who sometimes didn't have their parents with them. Very occasionally, a nurse would ask for a change if she found a particular patient difficult or felt she needed more experience in another field.

Henry came off the ventilator after twenty-four hours; he used to suck constantly on his dummy and would yell if it fell out of his mouth. Carol and I would smile as he screeched and race to pop it back into his mouth. He would suck it back in with a soft sigh, his rosebud-shaped lips blissfully closing round it. Henry loved having his soft, almost bald, head stroked and Carol would often sit by the bed and soothe him to keep him settled.

'Who's a bonny baby? Are you the most beautiful baby in the world?' she would coo at him and he would smile back at her, showing off his pink gums. I enjoyed Carol's company and she was very helpful, always asking what she could do to assist, but I also noticed that when she wasn't there I managed to work quietly and efficiently on my own. Each day I looked after Henry, I felt more equal to the task.

Carol was very anxious when, after a couple of days, we starting preparing for his chest drains to come out because she thought his breathing would be affected.

'Will he be okay? Will it hurt him? Will he still be able to breathe?' she asked a number of times.

'It might hurt a bit but it will be over very quickly. He'll be able to breathe fine, try not to worry,' I tried to reassure her.

Back in those days, we did not give routine pain relief, even to a small child like Henry. When the draining had stopped and a chest X-ray had been taken to ensure that his lungs were expanded, the doctors gave the go-ahead for the drains to be taken out.

When I talked to Carol about removing the chest drain I realised she thought it was going right into the lung and not into the cavity around the lung. Many people see their bodies as plumbing systems or a machine with parts and cavities are connected by pipes. The parents had already had the operation explained to them, with diagrams showing where the hole in the heart was and how it would be corrected. But parents, like Carol, are often so anxious that they cannot take it all in at first and it has to be explained a second or third time. So I found a piece of paper and a pencil and drew the lungs, and the lining covering them, in order to explain where the doctor had put the drains and why they were necessary – to drain any excessive blood or fluid which might collect and press on the lung, causing respiratory distress or infection.

'Ah, that's why you make him cough a lot and give him so much physio,' she said, finally understanding my explanation.

'Exactly!'

I felt good after this exchange, as I could see that it helped to reassure the mother about the care her child was receiving.

'I'll stay and comfort him,' Carol said, as we prepared Henry and the trolley before the procedure.

'Hold his arms and legs, to keep him as still as

you can,' I instructed her and the nurse helping me.

I cleaned his skin with Betadine, an iodine skin-cleansing agent, and prepared to remove both drains, one at a time. A silk tie was wrapped round the tube and passed through the skin, like a stitch, to keep it in place. Next, I unwrapped the tie and held it while I removed the drain, just as Henry was breathing out. I then quickly tied the silk stitch and applied a dressing over the wound to reduce the risk of air entry.

'Out it comes.' I tried to sound as confident and relaxed as possible. Henry started screaming, so Carol put the dummy in his mouth and cuddled him. She looked as if she had stopped breathing in anticipation. The procedure was painful but over in two seconds.

'All over,' I reassured them.


On the ward there was also a three-bedded intensive care unit and I was dreading going into this section. If my experience of a 'normal' ward was anything to go by, this was going to be an even greater challenge. I knew that as well as children having cardiac arrests, there were other emergencies to deal with, such as when the chest was opened up again on the ward after surgery if there wasn't time for the patient to be taken back to theatre. This usually happened if the heart needed massage or if the child was bleeding and a blood vessel needed to be tied off. During my time in intensive care, I knew I would be watched and mentored and wouldn't be moved on to more 'difficult' patients until my seniors felt I was ready, but it was still an extremely daunting prospect.

As time went on, I found the other staff and doctors very helpful and always ready to answer my questions. I began to grow in confidence, and started to look beyond my immediate jobs to see the ward as a whole.

The play staff were always keeping the children amused and I still found it astonishing that children were laughing, covering themselves in paint, and throwing toys around within a few days of being operated on.

Henry stayed with us for a total of ten days and I cared for him every day that I was on duty. The play leader had put a mobile with brightly coloured farm animals above his head. His mother would play with them to encourage him to look and would quietly talk to him, helping his development. Once all his drains were out, she would cuddle him on her lap and she enjoyed feeding him. Carol had continued expressing her breast milk with a pump in order to be able to do so. Initially Henry was fed through a naso-gastric tube directly into his stomach, but when he gradually began to nurse at her breast we gave only half the milk by tube; the rest he suckled, until he began slowly putting on weight. Carol was thrilled when this happened; because of his heart condition he had always been a slow feeder and she would sit patiently for hours while he drank. Now he seemed raring to go and would be full and burped after a matter of minutes.

When Henry was feeding properly and had gained enough weight, it was decided that he could go home. I felt a mixture of relief and quiet satisfaction that I had done a good job. I had grown fond of both Carol and Henry, but knew from my previous experience that it doesn't pay to get attached to the children one nurses. I had only been doing my job and we probably wouldn't keep in touch. I was just glad that Henry was happy and well enough to be going home. It was a good start to my time at GOSH and I felt optimistic about the months ahead.

As I saw Carol and Henry out of the hospital and headed back to the ward ready for my next challenge, a consultant was talking to one of the junior doctors in the corner of the room. They were flicking through medical notes and deep in discussion.

'Remember, the child's needs come first,' I overhead the consultant mutter. 'The child first and always.'

Little did I know then that this motto would sum up my long career at GOSH.

# 2

# Days in the Sluice

My story began like that of so many young girls in those days. I just knew, instinctively, that I wanted to be a nurse.

I left school in 1961 at the age of sixteen, with just two O level passes. My first job was at Marks & Spencer in Cambridge, where I lived with my mother, my father, Norman, and younger brother Peter. I worked behind the jumpers and cardigans counter for eighteen months, advising smart ladies on their jumpers and which colours suited their particular skin tone. I longed to graduate to what I considered the pinnacle of the department, the dress area where you could mingle amongst the hanging rows of expensive clothes, but never quite managed it. Every day, on the way to work, I travelled past the grand façade of Addenbrooke's Hospital and looked eagerly through the smeared bus window. The hospital was a real institution in the city and I knew that it was hugely respected. It always appeared busy, as people swept into the car park in their Cortinas and classic Minis. They rushed through the grey doorways, which appeared to swallow them up like a large mouth. There would always be nurses coming in and out, swarming like bees around patients, and they looked so regal in their smart uniforms. I really enjoyed my job at M&S, not least because I was earning some money and had access to the wonderful staff perks such as chiropody, having my hair done and being able to buy their food at a discount (a bonus for my family as we never had much money), but I knew it was just a stopgap. Nursing was my dream.

I finally plucked up courage to apply for the hospital's three-year nurses' training course, and a few weeks after submitting my application, I was delighted when I was called for an interview.

At that time, the strict, hierarchical system of nursing was still in force. Each hospital had a matron, who was the most senior nurse and responsible for all the staff – nursing, administrative and domestic – and also for standards of care and the general running of the different wards and departments. Everything that didn't fall under the medical umbrella was the matron's responsibility. I had heard many tales of terrifying and tyrannical matrons who, like dragons, ruled their staff with steely determination and rods of iron. The matron at Addenbrooke's was a tall, thin, grey-haired lady by the name of Miss Puddicombe, who I had learnt was both revered and feared in equal measure. During my interview she asked a few basic questions, which I initially answered nervously and with a stutter. However, I found her kind and fair and slowly relaxed and opened up as we talked. I came away thinking that I had done my best and could do no more, but I had my fingers and toes tightly crossed that things would go my way. I didn't know what I would do if I didn't make the grade.

A few days later, an ominous brown envelope fell through the letterbox and I rushed to rip it open before it had even hit the mat. I had been accepted on the nursing course! I was delighted, as were my mum and dad, and set about planning my new life away from home. I planned to work so hard that Florence Nightingale herself would have been proud of me!

When the time came, I handed in my notice at Marks & Spencer with mixed feelings. I left on a Friday and started at Addenbrooke's the following Monday. I woke that morning at 5 a.m. with terrible butterflies and spent the next two hours tossing and turning in my narrow bed, anxiously doing mental checklists to make sure I had packed everything I would need, from underwear to washing powder. I wouldn't be that far from our house, but it was still the first time I had lived away from home, and the thought of being totally self-sufficient both excited and terrified me. Although I had imagined it many times, I had no idea what to expect. As I ate breakfast, my porridge stuck in my throat like glue. Mum, Dad and my brother Peter tried to make me feel better as we sat around our kitchen table, eating our last meal together. Peter, who was only nine at the time, kept cracking jokes about my lack of cooking skills and how I would probably shrink all my clothes in the wash, but I failed to crack a smile. I was so nervous that my hands were trembling and my head was spinning.

The nurses' hostel was called Owlstone Croft and my room was basic, with a single divan bed that sank in the middle, a small cracked lamp, a wardrobe that had seen better days and a wooden desk with a chair. A brown rug covered the floor near the bed. There was a shared kitchen and bathroom, with several toilets for each corridor of ten rooms.

After my parents had helped to ferry my many belongings in overflowing cardboard boxes from the car to my room, and I had waved them off with plenty of hugs and promises to phone and write regularly, I sat down on my bed. Would I make friends? Would I make the grade? What if I wasn't any good at nursing? As I stared down at my feet I suddenly felt very homesick. I was already wearing the regulation footwear. I thought about my mum's reaction when I had pulled a face at the shoes when in the shop. She had laughed and told me, 'You'll be thankful for those shoes when you've been on your feet for twelve hours.'

Later on in life, I remember being appreciative of my mother's insistence on my not wearing high heels or tight shoes. Many people these days have bunions or crooked toes and suffer for having been a slave to fashion. I was very grateful to my mum for her wise words as I was constantly on my feet during my nursing career.

All the 'preliminaries', as we were called for the first six months, soon came together in the common room, and as I looked around, I was relieved to see that everyone looked terrified, especially a small mousy-haired girl who seemed to be fighting the urge to vomit. The warden, Miss Moore, was a sour-faced, whippet-thin spinster in her fifties, who peered at us through black-rimmed glasses. Her sidekick was a large lady who seemed much more reasonable and friendly and at least attempted a half-hearted smile. After some basic introductions and checks to make sure we were all present and correct, Miss Moore issued us with a long and strict list of instructions: preliminaries must be home by 10 p.m.; rooms must be kept tidy; no men would be allowed upstairs; preliminaries must look immaculate at all times ... the list went on and on and it was clear that we were expected to accept these instructions without argument. We were also expected to uphold the good name of the hospital and nursing at all times – day and night! A couple of the girls were reprimanded by Miss Moore for talking while she was speaking and I made a mental note to avoid her at all costs.

After she had left, telling us we had an hour until we were expected to be in bed, a voice piped up: 'Goodness, that Miss Moore talks a lot of tosh, doesn't she? Is there anything we *are* allowed to do?'

I looked round. Next to me stood a short and squat girl with a brown elfin-cut bob and a dirty laugh.

'Pleased to make your acquaintance,' she said, changing her thick Kentish accent into a distinctly smart London one. 'I'm Cathy.'

'Hi, I'm Susan. I'm glad you were thinking that too.'

'I daren't exhale in case it's not in the rule-book,' she said.

Cathy and I quickly bonded over the things we weren't allowed to do. She was a brilliant impersonator and went to great lengths to keep us all chuckling. My homesick feelings disappeared almost immediately. Some of the girls had been cadet nurses, a position for sixteen-year-olds who wanted to become nurses, and they regaled us with grim tales of the wards and what weird and wonderful things they had faced so far in their training. The new intake of nurses was grouped in what were known as 'sets'. We were the October '63 set.

The following day we were measured for our uniforms, which consisted of a lilac and white dress with thin straps, stiff white apron, collar and starched white hat, and we were given a four-hour lesson in 'how to make it up'. The hat was known as a 'butterfly' and it was a bit like origami; it wasn't at all easy to manipulate into the recommended shape. It needed several white hairgrips to keep it on your head and woe betide any young nurse whose hat slipped off! It took a number of practices before we were considered smart enough. The 'butterflies' often became quite grubby before we could find the time to make new ones, and it was not uncommon to be told off about 'the grey marks on your hat, nurse'. We had to wear our hair up under the hat at all times, with no wispy bits. And as for make-up, even a smudge of red lipstick or a brush of eyeshadow was out of the question, and we would be sent to the bathroom to wipe it off immediately. We weren't allowed to wear any jewellery; the only 'extra' permitted was a basic fob watch. We also had navy blue cloaks with a red lining and navy raincoats for wearing outdoors, along with an Addenbrooke's scarf, which was Cambridge blue, with mauve and white stripes.

Our seniority was indicated by the colour of our belts. The preliminaries had the same colour belt as their uniform, conveying no status at all. The second-year students had a dark purple stripe around the middle of their belts and the third-years had a purple belt. As a staff nurse, you wore a hat with a large white square with a flap down the back; by then you had made it, or so you thought! One of the traditional highlights was the wearing of a silver buckle on your belt when you qualified. A member of your family bought it for you and you sewed the stiff petersham band on to the buckle, like a watch onto its strap. Some buckles had been handed down through families for generations – they were considered a real mark of honour. I couldn't wait to get mine but I had a long way to go before then.

We were warned that if we didn't look pristine at all times, we would face Matron's wrath. And that felt like a terrifying prospect.

Dressing in my uniform for the first time was a

fantastic moment. It hung off me like the clothes I used to wear for school, which my mum bought a size too large, for me to 'grow into'. It wasn't the most comfortable attire, but I felt like I had finally arrived where I belonged. We soon learnt that the stiff, starched collars rubbed your neck raw so we would rub soap into the material, which helped.

'We scrub up quite well, don't we, Sue?' Cathy asked, as we stood in front of the mirror in the shared bathroom, admiring ourselves. I was beaming from ear to ear and felt really proud and excited. I couldn't wait to get started.

On my first day, as I stepped over the threshold into a world that was going to consume my life, I was utterly terrified. I felt so inadequate walking on to the ward and tried to blend into the background, constantly aware of minding my Ps and Qs. All the staff were rushing purposefully around, some deep in conversation about their work. Everywhere I looked there were sick people lying in bed – I remember thinking that no one must ever get better and go home.

On every ward, Sister was in charge and she was the equivalent of God. The senior staff nurse was next in the pecking order, followed by the junior staff nurses, then by the third-year, second-year and first-year students. Last of all came the 'prelims', who were officially the lowest of the low. I was in awe of the senior nurses and longed to be like them, with their assured air and confident manner. They seemed so knowledgeable.

The cleaners were the friends of the prelims; they were responsible for domestic duties, such as mopping floors, pulling out beds to clean behind them, washing the dishes and cleaning cubicles after patients were discharged. Finally, there was the ward clerk who did all the clerical work, such as preparing charts, answering the phone and so on. Busying themselves in the background, the clerks normally noticed everything and had the ear of Sister, so would faithfully report what they saw.

As prelims, we were told in no uncertain terms that it would take hard work, grit and sweat to rise through the ranks. Seniority was respected and etiquette considered paramount. We were always expected to open doors for older members of staff and speak only when spoken to. If any impudent young nurse stepped out of line, she was immediately marched to the office to be given a dressing-down. Junior and senior staff never mixed outside the ward, except on rare occasions. The doctors had their own dining room, as did the sisters, and in the main dining room, junior nurses never mixed with staff nurses. Everyone had their place and ours was well and truly on the bottom rung of the ladder.

Consultants were the absolute top of the ranking system and masters of their domain. Even Sister kowtowed to them, making sure they had everything they needed during the daily ward rounds and trotting after them to answer any questions. Sandwiches and pots of tea were made for them beforehand and when this practice was stopped many years later, all hell was let loose! Some consultants put on a show by talking loudly about various complicated diagnoses, especially if we were in the lift with them. A stream of dishevelled and exhausted-looking junior doctors would often follow in their wake, with their hair askew, their skin washed out and their eyes gummy from lack of sleep.

There was a huge drama before each consultant's visit: we would rush around, cleaning and mopping, until everything was gleaming, so much that you could virtually see your face in the bedpans. Then, just before the consultant's arrival, we would skitter out of sight, as if we had never been there at all. On the odd occasion when a consultant arrived on the ward without warning, everyone would take a sharp, collective intake of breath and pray he didn't ask any important questions.

I vividly remember an occasion when I'd just done a routine bedpan round and I was carrying a particularly smelly one, without a lid, to the sluice. As I walked along the corridor, somebody somewhere must have opened a door or window, as there was a rush of breeze which picked up some of the dirty toilet paper from my pan and swept it into the air with a whoosh, only to land at the feet of one of the consultants, an extremely tall and rakish gentleman who was marching past with a purposeful look about him.

'Gosh, I'm so sorry, I'm so sorry,' I said, dropping on my hands and knees to remove the offending article.

He looked down at me, raised one bushy eyebrow and continued on his way without saying a word. From then on, I made sure that every bedpan I removed had a lid on it. When I relayed the story to Cathy later, she made me repeat it three times, so delighted was she at my humiliation.

My first ward was Griffiths Ward, the men's medical, which had patients with cardiac failure, strokes, renal and liver failure, respiratory infections and skin diseases. Some patients had cancer and others were undergoing terminal care. The sister, Sister Griffiths – they were known by the name of the ward – who was in her fifties and tall, with a big bust and dark, pulled-back hair, reminded me of my grandmother. She fussed about the patients and gave them plenty of attention, fluffing up their pillows and hanging on their every word – they really loved her. She demanded respect but if we prelims did what she asked, she was fair with us, and I slowly became less terrified as the days went by.

In the first few weeks I was mainly confined to the sluice, cleaning and sterilising bedpans, urinals and vomit bowls. Everything needed to be boiled clean, including the cheatles forceps, which were used for taking the equipment out of the boiler. These were kept in a large container in Savlon disinfectant to prevent cross-infection. The smell of disinfectant seemed to cling to my skin for days and lodge itself up my nostrils. As my glasses were always steaming up, I seemed to live in a constant mist and was forever taking them off to wipe them free of condensation.

We learnt about measuring and testing urine for sugar, albumen, ketones and blood; if it was cloudy or smelt fishy, this would indicate an infection. We had to examine stools: Were they loose in texture, constipated, black, brown, pale coloured? Did the faeces contain blood, mucus or any undigested food, or even worms? All this information was recorded on the patients' fluid charts; it was imperative to report anything abnormal. If we were lucky, we were allowed out of the sluice to do the locker round, which involved cleaning and tidying the lockers in which patients kept things like jewellery (no locked cupboards in those days) and toiletries. We also had to empty their sputum or vomit pots, and then sterilise the pots in the sluice. Everywhere was to be kept clean at all times, without a speck of dust in sight.

Sometimes, when we were filling the steriliser with water in the sluice, we would be called away to do something more important. More often than not the job would take longer than expected, or another person would attract our attention and we'd forget we had left the tap on. The sluice flooded a number of times and water flowed into the ward or dripped down to the ward below. We would hastily put sheets and bundles of towels on the floor to soak it up and our shoes would get drenched as we waded through the water to turn the tap off. There were a number of first-years, including me, who managed to commit this same misdemeanour during the early weeks of training, much to Sister Griffiths' annoyance.

'Girls, WHO left the tap on AGAIN?' she would yell, as we all cowered before her, trying to work back through the jobs we had done to figure out who was the culprit.

It was the sputum pots that used to make me want to vomit. During my first month, a man who had cancer of the lung coughed up a lot of sputum, and then accidentally knocked the pot from the side of the locker on to the floor. I thought I was going to be sick there and then, but I took a deep breath and managed to control myself as I wiped it up. Afterwards I was grateful for the privacy of the sluice, where I retched a few times before getting a grip on myself.

Bed-making was also an art to be perfected. The beds had to be neatly aligned and we had to make them up with traditional 45-degree 'hospital corners', where the sheet was folded and tucked under the mattress in a straight line. Old habits die hard and I still make up my bed at home in this way.

We were constantly making sure that water jugs were refilled and the amount drunk charted appropriately and that flower vases were topped up. Every patient seemed to have about two or three and these had to be taken out of the ward at night and put back again in the morning. To this day, I do not see the logic of this practice, other than that the flowers at least had their water changed on a daily basis.

Other duties involved helping with such patient care as giving bed baths and relieving pressure areas – on the buttocks, shoulders, heels, elbows, knees – for bedridden patients, and giving out bedpans and urinals at the appropriate times. This was a basic part of patient care, as was lubricating and cleaning the mouths of patients who were unable to eat and drink. Some would have a naso-gastric tube, known as a Ryle tube, which passed through the nose to the stomach, either to feed them or to drain their stomachs through aspiration. First, we had to check that the tube was in the stomach by aspirating some stomach contents and testing these with litmus paper. If blue litmus paper turned pink, indicating acid, then the tube was considered to be in the stomach. If not, we would get it checked by a more senior nurse and sometimes had to insert another tube. This was most uncomfortable for the patient.

It was a very steep learning curve. The first bed bath I ever gave was to a man who was really thin, having lost a lot of weight. I was terrified that if I lifted his arm to sponge it down, I would knock everything out of line. My own arm was quivering so much that he must have been scared himself!

There were frequent tears shed in the privacy of the sluice, as sharp words were said by Sister if we did not live up to the standards required. I often found myself with hot tears running down my cheeks after being shouted at to hurry, when I was already working as fast as I could manage. On more than one occasion, I also found myself frustrated when I forgot something, such as charting a patient's urine output. Sometimes Sister made me double-check a urine sample and the result would always be the same. I felt exasperated but didn't dare to answer back.

I had to toughen up quickly. I remember that the first dead body I saw was on Griffiths Ward. A man had died of a stroke. The staff nurse asked if I would like to help her 'lay out the body'. I jumped at the chance, eager to experience something that I knew would be a regular part of my life as a nurse, although I hoped not *too* regular. I had many items to tick off in my Pink Syllabus Book of nursing procedures, in which I had to prove myself competent, and this was one of them. The book provided basic information on which the pattern of training for registration with the General Nursing Council for England and Wales is planned. The subjects included caring for patients after IV (intravenous) therapy, setting up for a lumbar puncture, giving a bed bath, applying a dressing, and so on, and each had to be signed off by sisters and tutors.

When I went into the room where the dead man was to be laid out, there was an eerie silence, and of course I felt a little anxious. In one corner there was a trolley with all the necessary things, like cotton wool to pack the orifices, forceps, scissors, a shroud, sheets, safety pins, bandages to tie the feet together, a washbowl with cloths and the relevant paperwork to pin to the body. At the other side of the room lay the dead body, covered in a sheet. The window had been opened and the curtain blew in the wind. When the staff nurse lifted the sheet back gently and respectfully, I didn't know what to expect – the man's face was pale, with blue lips, but had a serene and peaceful expression. I soon got over my fear and learnt to do the last offices for this poor man. When he was turned so that we could wash his back, I heard air come out of his mouth in a puff, like a sigh. The staff nurse explained that this often happened when moving a dead body.

When we had finished, the man's relatives would be allowed in to pay their last respects. I was grateful that I wouldn't have to show them in because I am sure I would have burst into tears. I hated showing my emotions, especially in front of others.

It was important to learn the correct way to talk to patients, to find out how they were feeling and how we could make them comfortable: the very essence of being a nurse. Most of the patients on Griffiths Ward were happy to have a familiar face around and just wanted to chat about the news and what we nurses had been doing in our free time, but this didn't go down very well with the various sisters. 'Stop gossiping, Nurse Macqueen, and get on with your work!' I would often be told by Sister.

Dealing with patients was, oddly, more complex than it sounds. While I was on the ward for men with renal failure during my first year, I was giving a man a sponge bath to try and bring his temperature down. He was aged about thirty and very good-looking with a chiselled jaw and bright blue eyes. As I methodically and silently went over his chest and arms with cool water, he looked at me playfully.

'Enjoying that, aren't you, Nurse?' he said with a wink.

Was this a chat-up line or did he just mean was I enjoying my work? My heart started beating just that little bit faster and I know I blushed. The men loved teasing the nurses.

'I really enjoy caring for patients,' I answered, with a wry smile, and swiftly moved on to the next patient.

Some of the men were really naughty. In the orthopaedic ward, the male patients were mostly young and had been operated on for broken bones sustained in motorbike accidents, and so on, whereas the female patients tended to be elderly with broken hips. This ward was much livelier than the others and its inhabitants were renowned for being mischievous. Once there was a young man who had been in hospital for a few weeks with a broken leg and he had picked up an infection. He was short and stout and had brightly coloured tattoos all the way up his arms. His broken leg was on traction, with pins through it to try and straighten it out, and a system of weights and pulleys to hold it in position while it healed. He was clearly frustrated and would regularly bellow, 'Nurse, Nurse, I'm bored!'

I was going about my duties on that particular day when he called me over.

'How can I help?' I asked, as I neared the bed.

'Come here,' he said and I moved a few steps closer. As I did so he grabbed me with both arms and pulled me on top of him in a flash of colour and sweat. I fell into him and my uniform rode right up and my hat was knocked crooked. I felt the blood rush to my head.

'Ay, ay. Fancy a bit of me, do you?' He laughed as I attempted to pull myself off him.

'Really, sir . . .' I stammered.

Just at that moment Sister Giles, a young married lady with a knowing smile, appeared by my side.

'Nurse Macqueen, what *are* you doing?' she cried, a look of horror on her face. I'm sure she had seen incidents like this many times before, but at the time I was mortified.

During the training years, we rotated around the many wards at Addenbrooke's, such as Albert (male surgery), Paget (female medical), Thackeray (radiotherapy) and Bowtell (men's genito-urinary surgery). On Bowtell Ward, the sister was particularly strict. When giving a report on handover, she would expect us to know the names of all twenty-five patients, their diagnosis, date of operation, whether they had passed urine, their temperature, and any abnormalities. I had been used to reading this information out from our Kardex – the nursing notes of all the patients. In doing so, I often overlooked some piece of information and she would remind me in no uncertain terms that I must know all these details off by heart. I was so nervous that I would go bright red when she put me on the spot and almost always forget some other detail, despite spending hours trying to memorise everything perfectly.

'Nurse Macqueen, if I've told you once, I've told you ten times, you must know this information OFF BY HEART,' she would bark.

'Yes, Sister,' I would squeak back, giving myself a mental kick in the shins, as the fact invariably would then find its way to the tip of my tongue.

There were also more formal studies, including human biology, physiology, anatomy and nutrition. We spent a lot of our time off studying together in our sets and Cathy and I attempted to make this at least vaguely enjoyable. I have always tried my best to knuckle down to authority, whereas Cathy was more interested in gossiping and making everyone chuckle.

We sat both written and practical exams in huge

classrooms with cupboards full of shiny instruments and complicated equipment. We would be asked by the tutor to lay up a trolley for a procedure such as a dressing or an intravenous insertion, and then have to talk through how we would do it and what the complications might be. Sometimes, we had to test urine and identify the abnormalities, so we had to know our physiology as well as anatomy. There would be Bunsen burners and chemical mixtures such as Esbach's solution, which was used for detecting albumen in urine. If we were doing well, the examiners would change the subject and try to catch us out – at least that is how it felt. There were usually two tutors and they would switch over asking questions at half-time. The tests got longer and more complex as we became more senior. Books such as *Anatomy and Physiology for Nurses* by Sears and *The Principles and Practice of Surgical Nursing* by Nash, *Modern Nursing: Theory and Practice* by Winifred Hector and *Medicine for Nurses* by Toohey became our bibles and our bedtime reading.

We were certainly working hard, but this also meant playing hard and we had a fantastic social life. We had to be back at Owlstone Croft by 10 p.m., but we could obtain a late pass from Matron's office so long as we were not on duty early the next morning, and after we had been quizzed sufficiently about our motives for being out late. However, we soon found ways around this. The other girls and I would creep out past Miss Moore's office after dinner and come back long past our 10 p.m. curfew. There were certain ways of avoiding her, including giving each other a leg-up through open windows on the ground floor. Once we were even forced to form a human pyramid in order to make it back to our rooms. Cathy insisted that as she was lightest she should go on top, but I wasn't so sure! There was always plenty of suppressed laughter. Many a time Miss Moore tried to catch us out, but much to our delight she never quite managed it. Cathy and I loved pulling our hair into a bun and asking each other, in our finest Miss Moore voice: 'What are you doing, Nurse?'

'Studying, Miss Moore,' we would reply in unison, doubling over with laughter.

From our first night at the nurses' home, she remained frosty and strict and we went out of our way to give her a wide berth.

However, I remember a tragic incident when a girl sustained a serious head injury when she jumped out of a second-floor window to go to a party. An ambulance soon arrived on the scene and the police were called and asked lots of questions. Miss Moore was mortified and, for once, I felt quite sorry for her. The girl was never the same after that and had to give up nursing. I never knew her personally, but the incident shocked us all; it was so real and far too close for comfort.

Along with dodging Miss Moore, we also had to make sure we avoided the portly university proctors, who would prowl the streets at night with their dogs to check for errant students. We could hear them striding around a mile off and would run in the opposite direction as fast as our heels could carry us.

Nurses weren't allowed to enter the doctors' residential staff quarters, unless it was to get a prescription signed at night, and with the permission of the night sister. Everyone wanted to catch a doctor and the nurses and junior doctors were always having fun together, with the grapevine keeping everyone informed of who was going out with whom, when, where and how. It seemed as though nothing was kept secret. There was a surgical registrar we all fancied called Norman, whose every movement – almost down to his most recent visit to the toilet – was the grapevine's lifeblood. He had sandy-coloured hair with a reddish tinge and was strapping because he played rugby in his free time. He reminded me of a Hollywood movie star like Robert Redford and we would all daydream wistfully about him. It was all just fun though; it wasn't the done thing to get married when you were still training. I think the powers that be thought the strain of caring for patients *and* a husband was beyond us! In those days, married women, especially those with children, invariably stayed at home and cared for their family.

Many of us found boyfriends in the form of handsome junior doctors and students from the university, and there was a never-ending list of parties to attend. One night, about three months into my first year, Cathy took me to a gathering at a flat of one of the older nurses she knew. I was exhausted after a long day on my feet, but it only took her a few minutes to persuade me to go along.

'C'mon, Sue. Don't be a spoilsport. She's promised that loads of handsome men from the university will be there. We'll just go for an hour and then you can have your six hours' beauty sleep!'

I shook off my uniform, pulled on my favourite dress and told her I'd meet her outside. Successfully navigating my escape past Miss Moore, half an hour later we arrived, rung the bell and a young man with a chocolate-coloured pencil moustache opened the door.

'Hi,' he said shyly. There was a long and slightly awkward pause.

'Erm, we're here for the party. Are you going to leave us outside all day?' Cathy demanded. 'We've even brought a bottle,' she added, waving it up and down.

'Oh, gosh, sorry, yes, do come in,' he replied, glancing down.

'Sorry about her,' I said, as Cathy bounded up the stairs with me struggling to keep up.

The living room in the girl's flat was filled with smoke and couples dancing and pressed up against the walls. There was a bowl of punch in the corner, which tasted as though every last bit of alcohol the hosts could lay their hands on had been emptied into it. Music by artists like The Beatles, Elvis Presley, Cliff Richard and The Shadows and Buddy Holly was blaring from a vinyl record player.

Later, as I stood in the kitchen nursing my third glass of the rather dodgy punch and wondering where Cathy had got to, the man who had opened the door reappeared.

'Hi, I'm William,' he said hesitantly. 'You're the one with the ... erm ... loud friend?'

'Yes, that's one way of putting it. I'm Susan.'

William was a marginally taller than my five-foot-five and studying at St John's College. He filled me in with tales of the eccentric teaching staff and their heavy workload. As I prepared to leave, he asked if he could take me to the pictures the following Friday and I happily accepted.

I don't remember being mad about William as he was very serious-minded and seemed quite nervous at first when we were alone together. I sensed I was his first girlfriend, but I was definitely happy to have a steady boyfriend like some of the others, especially on the nights when a group of us would go to one of the local pubs or the packed university union bars at each college where the drinks were cheaper.

We certainly didn't spend much time at the hostel and we were always running short of money. I was only earning a measly eleven pounds a month, which didn't stretch very far with all the socialising we did. So we were only too glad of the hospital canteen where we went for lunch or dinner, depending on what shift we were on, even though the meals were reminiscent of school dinners.

It was certainly work hard, play hard, but sometimes nurses would get ill and be sent off to the sick bay which was attached to the Thomas Potter Ward on the top floor of the hospital. They would be admitted only if absolutely necessary, but once inside, the elderly ward sister would fuss over her charges, giving them lots of pillows and hot drinks. She would even break the hospital rules about visitors, so they didn't get lonely and bored. I was never unwell enough to go up there, despite sometimes feeling so tired that I longed to be ill and have my pillows plumped and cups of tea made for me.

Each year we were required to do a number of night-duty shifts, which would be preceded by a handover, when the day staff would report on each patient, especially those needing special attention. Patients going to theatre in the morning would be 'nil by mouth', meaning they weren't allowed to eat or drink anything before an operation. In a spirit of camaraderie, we would leave notes for each other, saying 'Sister doesn't like you making a noise with the bedpans', 'Sister is very particular that our hats are pristine', or 'Make sure the beds are straight!'

On every ward there was a kitchen and during our night shift duty, on the rare occasions when things were quiet, we would cook dinner for each other, simple meals like ham, egg and chips. Sometimes we even found matching cutlery for the occasion. I remember one night, when one of the consultants – a squat and austere gentleman who clearly enjoyed his food – made a surprise visit. On entering the ward looking as if he was about to say something deeply profound, he took a deep inhalation through his large Roman nose and exclaimed, 'Something smells nice! Mmmmm.' His shirt buttons strained, showing flashes of pinky flesh.

I wasn't quite sure whether it was correct etiquette to offer him some of our makeshift meal or to hide all evidence of it.

I also recall an elderly South African man who was in the private ward on bed rest after suffering from a heart attack. As he was about six foot eight his feet would dangle over the end of his bed and he would need an extra blanket to cover them. He would beg us to go and talk to him at night and sometimes we would sit around gossiping with him during our breaks.

'I'm so lonely, Nurse Macqueen. Come and talk to me,' he would say. 'I need to know the latest instalment of gossip. All the patients here are so boring! And my radio crackles all the time.'

Our patient must have had hollow legs because he was always saying he was hungry. One night when we were sitting at his bedside, I had an idea. Sometimes one of the others would go and get some takeaway food.

'I could go and get us a curry,' I suggested. 'That new place around the corner is supposed to be really good. I could murder a beef vindaloo.'

As welcome as the hospital food was, everything tasted the same and was cooked within an inch of its life.

I dashed round to the curry house and ordered piles of takeaway: enough bhajis, naan bread, rice and vindaloos to blow our heads off. I raced back and we all sat together, peeling off the foil lids and getting stuck in. The food was luke warm by then, but no one seemed to mind. We got the patient's transistor radio going and The Beatles' 'Love, Love Me Do' rang out. It was like a proper party.

About five minutes into our spicy feast, the night sister, an Irish lady who was very kind and full of fun, stuck her head around the door.

'Nurses, I'm going to pretend that I haven't seen what is going on, but I wanted to let you know that the consultant is coming in with a patient shortly,' she told us. 'So if you were eating, say, a curry, you'd need to get rid of it sharpish.'

We knew the doctor would make a fuss as the man whose room we were in was one of his patients.

The spicy smell was overwhelming, so we hurried to open the window despite the cold night air and gave extra blankets to the patient. He thought it was hilarious and chuckled from his bed as we rushed nervously around the room.

'Oh girls, this is the best fun I've had in ages,' he said with a laugh.

'Start fanning,' someone yelled, so I picked up a spare pillow and started trying to circulate the air towards the window. By the time the consultant entered the ward, we were all busying ourselves elsewhere, the patient was pretending to be asleep, and the only giveaway was the faint smell of onion bhajis.

No wonder the patient complained that sleep evaded him at night. His notes always read, 'Asleep all day . . .'

Another time when I was on night duty it was one of the nurses' birthdays. She was very sporty, always off to play tennis or netball or to go running after work, and put the rest of us slightly to shame, so we decided on a novel way to test her endurance.

When things had quietened down on the ward after the initial rush, a number of us surprised her by man-handling her, fully clothed in her uniform, into an ice-cold bath, which had been lovingly prepared in advance.

'Let's see how well you hold up in this cold water,' someone yelled.

There was a nurse on lookout for the night sister, and the few patients who were in on the joke thoroughly enjoyed seeing us manoeuvre her down the middle of the ward to the bathroom. Fortunately, the birthday girl saw the funny side of it and when the night sister noted her absence, we reported that she had gone off duty early, not feeling well at all.

'She said she had the beginnings of a horrible cold, Sister,' someone piped up as we all bit down hard on our lips to stop ourselves laughing. If a nurse were to play a similar prank today they would be disciplined, but it was all good clean fun then. It also helped to release the tension of the day.

# 3

# Making a Difference

Life as a first-year student was fun and William and I continued dating for a couple of months. He would often show up at Owlstone Croft and leave some flowers with one of the other girls or Miss Moore, who called him, 'that young gentleman'. He was polite to a tee and it seems that despite his retiring personality, he had said something to charm her. Cathy was less impressed and called him 'stuffy'. William certainly wasn't the love of my life and I always had half an eye open for someone more fun-loving, but I enjoyed his easy company.

Our early shifts ran from 7 a.m. to 4 p.m., and the later ones from 1 p.m. to 10 p.m. On some days we did a split shift, which involved working from 7 a.m. to 2 p.m. and having a break, before going on duty from 5 p.m. through to 9 p.m. These shifts were always a bit of a killer as you felt as if you had been on your feet all day, but I tried to make the most of the time I had off in the middle of the day.

One day when I had a split shift, William happened to have a break in his lectures so we decided to go punting on the River Cam. William was in charge and I was relaxing with my feet up, enjoying a well-earned rest. He had been picked for the *University Challenge* team to go on TV – an accolade indeed – and was furiously absorbing as many facts as he could. I couldn't wait to see him on my small television screen in black and white.

It was a fine spring day and there were a few tourists around, but it was relatively quiet on the river. I had brought along a quiche I had made and some Coca-Cola, which was as popular then as it is now. There was no question of drinking alcohol when I knew I had to go back on duty. Even so, we had a fun afternoon in the pale sunshine, laughing and joking as we drifted from Jesus Green to Silver Street, past the imposing buildings of King's, Trinity and Queen's College.

'Which of Shakespeare's plays is the only one set in Vienna and in which the city's Duke adopts a disguise in order to observe the actions of his subjects, including his deputy, Angelo?' I asked, my eyes firmly on the answer. I wouldn't last five minutes on *University Challenge* but didn't want to give myself away.

'*Twelfth Night?*' William asked hopefully. 'No, no, *Measure for Measure.*'

'I'm afraid, St John's Cambridge, I'm going to have to take your first answer. You are wrong – the answer is *Measure for Measure.*'

'I said that!' he chuckled, stroking his fashionable moustache. 'You, Sue, are a hard taskmaster.'

He moved towards me, settling his arm across my shoulders, but I shrugged him off. I was starting to feel that maybe he was taking the relationship more seriously than I was. I wanted my life outside work to be about having fun, rather than having romantic meals and intimate moments together, and I felt that perhaps the time had come to let it slowly fizzle out.

As we drew up to the wooden punt station and I gingerly stepped ashore, hoisting my nurse's uniform up with one hand, I missed my footing and slipped, landing with a splash back into the dirty water. It was only up to my knees but very muddy.

'Agggh, I'm soaked! It's in my shoes!' I yelled.

'Oh Sue, here, take this.' William rushed to help me out and attempted to dry me off with his jumper, trying to suppress his laughter. But it was no use; I was sodden.

'That is doing absolutely nothing, William. Oh no, what am I going to do? This is a disaster!'

'Oh Sue, it would only happen to you,' he chuckled, rubbing harder with the jumper.

We couldn't stop giggling, but I was also panicking because I didn't have time to return to the hostel for a change of uniform.

'I need to be back at work in ten minutes, William, what if Sister sees me? There will be hell to pay'.

'Don't worry, Sue. You'll be okay.'

As he was talking, I was already scurrying off, the image of Sister's horrified face uppermost in my mind.

I rushed back to the hospital, praying that no one would see me as I hurried down to the musty basement where we had our lockers with all our belongings. Luckily I had another spare uniform stashed away and I quickly dressed, throwing my wet clothes to the bottom of the locker, to be dealt with later. For the rest of the day, my shoes squelched and I left suspicious wet footprints as I walked up and down the pristine ward. The cleaner kept looking at me with beady eyes, but I pretended that everything was completely normal.

Towards the end of my first year, I was on Paget, the female medical ward, and I was on night duty again. It was 9 p.m. and I had just taken handover with the day nurses. It was my first time on night duty for a week and I was tired, having been up most of the day. I was still finding it hard to readjust my body clock.

As I turned to get the Kardex book containing all the patients' nursing notes, I heard a hard, brittle voice from the corner of the room.

'Hello, Susan.'

I glanced up to see a familiar face looking up at me from one of the beds. I blinked twice and then realised: it was my old headteacher, Miss White. She had grey roots now, but the telltale red tinge of her hair remained, as did the hard expression. She was propped up in bed in a white, lacy nightie and was wearing an oxygen mask. I later learnt that she had been admitted to the hospital with cardiac problems.

Just eighteen months earlier, I had found myself outside Miss White's office, waiting to discuss what career I was going to pursue. I was fifteen and midway through my dreaded O levels, the time when the school started directing us towards what they thought were suitable careers. In the early 1960s, most young girls went into occupations such as nursing or teaching. At that time, no one at my school talked about going to university.

I was determined to be a nurse, no matter what. There was one girl at school, with an alabaster skin, who was always empathetic towards people who felt unwell; she would take small children by the hand to the school nurse when they fell over, and administered Band-Aids from her pockets at every opportunity. I remember thinking that I would never be a born nurse, like her, but my heart was set on nursing.

My father was in the Royal Navy and we moved around a lot with his work. We mostly lived in places along the south coast like Portsmouth, Lee-on-Solent and Gosport. Dad was an officer in the Navy and after the war he went into recruitment, although I liked to tell people when they asked that 'Dad won the war'! I loved the smart blue uniform which he wore with such pride. My mother had done a bit of basic auxiliary nursing in the past and she and Dad were very supportive of my desire to be a nurse. We were a working-class family of modest means, but we never went without. During my early childhood, the coupon system introduced during the war was still in place, but Dad would sometimes bring home big chunks of meat – I have no idea where they came from. Mum would rustle up huge pearl-barley stews and delicious roast dinners, and we would all sit round the dinner table together to enjoy them.

I attended ten different schools between the ages of five and sixteen, but we had settled in Cambridge by the time I was thirteen. I grew quite used to being the new girl and was never unhappy at school because I made friends easily. However, the standards varied from school to school and even though I was never particularly academic, I would often find myself daydreaming at the back of the class because I already knew what we were being taught. I never considered for a moment that I might not do well enough in my studies to pursue a nursing career.

When my turn came to be called into the dusty office and I duly sat before her, Miss White peered at me through her half-glasses over what I imagined to be a pile of very important, secret documents covered in red biro marks. She was small with scraped-back, dyed red hair. Cold and stiff, she could almost freeze mercury with a glance.

'Susan, what do you want to do when you finish your education?' she asked.

'I would really like to be a nurse,' I said, full of conviction and trying not to fidget or fiddle with my skirt, one of Miss White's pet hates.

'Hmm,' she paused for a few seconds, shuffling the notes in her hand. 'And why is that?'

'Well, I think I'd enjoy it and I like to think that maybe I could make a difference to some people ...'

'Well. I don't think that will be an option. I don't think you'll make the grade.'

'But why?' I asked, somewhat crestfallen, but not really all that surprised at her blunt response.

'Your grades aren't good enough.'

'But ...'

'Please call in Carolyn as you go out,' she said and returned to her red scribbling. The conversation was clearly over and she hadn't suggested anything else. But I didn't want to do anything else. There was no Plan B.

If anything, our encounter had made me more determined than ever. I thought, I'm still going to try. I'm going to do this.

Back on Paget Ward, it did flash through my mind that I should say something to Miss White about having become a nurse despite the fact that she had denounced me as not being bright enough. But the thought disappeared as quickly as it had arrived and I smiled at her instead.

'Miss White, how are you?'

She reached to move the oxygen mask off her mouth and I saw that her thin lips were slightly blue.

'Oh, not too bad, my dear, you know. Can't complain.' Her face broke into a faint, if slightly awkward, smile.

'I never thought, well ...' she trailed off. She looked weary and unwell.

I set about helping her, giving her a bedpan, taking her blood pressure and making sure she had everything she needed. It was a strange reversal of roles. As I left the cubicle she held my arm in a vice-like grip.

'Thank you, dear,' she said. 'You're very kind.'

'My pleasure,' I grinned back, satisfied and quietly triumphant.

As we moved into the second year, our duties increased and we cheerfully bequeathed our cleaning chores to subsequent intakes of student nurses. This enabled us to do other things, such as giving injections, taking blood, setting up drips with the doctor and applying dressings. I remember that we used to take great pride in doing urinary catheter care. This involved cleaning round the end of the penis where the catheter was inserted into the bladder, then wrapping a clean piece of gauze around it, neatly tied off with a bow! We liked to think we could inject a 'girlie' touch.

As time passed, I had to spend more time studying, as exams always seemed to be looming. Anatomy and physiology were my weak points and I tried to memorise facts by repeating them over and over again. There seemed to be so much to learn and I struggled to keep the information in my head. We would test one another out of the textbooks and the only time I felt confident was when I was asking the questions.

We had to master subjects like diabetes and be able to tell the difference between hyperglycaemia (too much sugar in the blood) and hypoglycaemia (too much insulin or not enough sugar in the blood), and how you treated the different conditions. It was complex and time-consuming and the facts seemed to spill out of my head as quickly as I ingested them, like an over-full bucket.

My first experience of giving someone an injection was certainly memorable. It was an antibiotic and I was trying my hardest to be calm and relaxed and go through the motions as if I had done it many times before. Supervised by a senior nurse, I drew up the injection with a dark green sterile needle in the treatment room. As I had rehearsed, I methodically put the sterile glass syringe, alcohol swab and cotton wool ball into the tray and, with the drug chart, took them to the patient's bedside. I checked his name band and his hospital number against the prescription sheet to ensure that the right patient was getting the right drug.

'Please can you turn over?' I asked. I was to give the injection into the man's buttock.

'This is Nurse Macqueen's first injection. Are you happy for her to do it?' my tutor asked the man, as I carefully washed my hands.

'Yes, that's fine,' he said as he turned away from me with his large posterior in the firing line. I couldn't see the expression on his face.

I took a deep breath and mentally drew a cross on his right buttock, as I knew I had to give the injection in the upper outer quadrant of the muscle to avoid the sciatic nerve and the bone. As I had been taught, I cleaned the skin with the alcohol swab and let it dry, taking deep breaths all the while. Then I took the glass syringe from the tray, checked there was no air in the syringe and held it so that I could 'dart it' into the skin. As I did so, time seemed to stand still ... the needle bounced back without piercing the skin! I quickly realised that I had forgotten to say 'Take a deep breath' to relax the patient and his muscle was tense. I glanced at my supervisor who had her mouth open in an 'O' shape and I felt the blood rushing up my neck. Then I asked him to relax and quickly tried again.

I was careful to ensure that the needle did not go in up to the hilt, as this is where it could break if the patient moved suddenly, leaving the needle inside him – a major complication. I pulled the plunger of the syringe back a little to ensure that the needle was not in a blood vessel, injected the fluid, then slowly withdrew the needle, put the cotton wool ball over the site and rubbed gently. It was over, the first of thousands of injections I knew I would have to give during my career. And it was hopefully the first and last time that the needle would bounce back out again.

'Thank you, Nurse, that was very good,' the man said, pulling up his pants. I knew he wasn't telling the truth, but I happily initialled the prescription sheet and returned the tray to the drug room. I was shaking with adrenalin. I had given my first injection. I couldn't wait to tell my friends all about it.

By this time I had moved into a maisonette at No. 19 Bateman Street with three other nurses, Marion, Farida and Linda.

Sadly, Cathy had failed her first-year exams and decided that nursing wasn't for her.

'I need to earn some proper money, not clean up vomit,' she had said before heading home to Essex and promising to write. After an initial burst of correspondence – she eventually became a teacher – sadly we lost touch as the years went by. I still think about her witty personality and the fun we had in that first year.

Marion, Linda and I were in the same set, while Farida was in the set above us. Linda was a black-belted judo expert, who kept her judo kit on top of her bed because she said it 'gave her strength'. Farida was an Indian girl from a wealthy family from East Africa, who owned a chain of shoe shops, and Marion an easy-going girl who eventually married a man she met during our student days. Through Farida and her cousin Rashida we became friendly with another group of nurses in their set who shared a flat on nearby Marshall Road. The nurses who lived there were Marianne, Valerie (we called her Cuth because her surname was Cuthbert), Netty and Pat Pond (we called her Pondso). We three remain friends almost fifty years later, but I have lost touch with Marianne, as well as Rashida and Linda. I was sad to learn that Farida passed away some years ago.

Our flat was a grotty old place, but at least we could afford it. On the first floor was a large kitchen which looked as if it hadn't been cleaned for years. In the sitting room there was a threadbare carpet with a couple of moth-eaten sofas and a three-bar gas fire on which we used to toast marshmallows. There was no central heating, of course. There were two bedrooms on the top floor, which we had to share, and it was so cold in the winter months that we put newspaper between the sheets to try and keep warm. The inside of the windows would sometimes frost up during the coldest days. But despite our dingy home, life was fun and relatively carefree, we had many, many parties with plenty of bottles of cheap and cheerful plonk and dancing until the small hours, even when reporting for duty at 7 a.m. We took great delight in trying the latest fashions and would often spend our days off trawling through the local charity shops looking for the perfect garish creation.

By then, I had split up with William. A few months into our romance, before he went home for the long summer holidays, I had told him that I was too busy with my work to go on seeing him. This was not really true but I wanted to let him down gently. We continued to have fun with the boys at the university colleges and there seemed to be no end to the invitations. No wonder we were permanently tired; a late shift followed by a party, followed by an early shift, was not uncommon. Some days on the ward, I was so exhausted that I went about my duties in an almost robotic way, counting down the hours until I could lie down and close my eyes.

We were extremely trusting in those days and came and went as we pleased, leaving the door on the latch. One evening I was having an early night, which for us was about 10 p.m. I had a long day at work ahead of me and that night was the start of the annual May Balls, which was always a late affair. The others were staying up to see the results of the 1964 general election, when Harold Wilson became Labour prime minister. I put my curlers in my hair, changed into a clean nightie before arranging my bedclothes, with newspaper between the covers for warmth, and gratefully climbed underneath. I went to sleep immediately; it was such a luxury that I never had trouble getting off. Some time later, I was roused from slumber by someone stroking my foot with brittle fingers and I thought it must my room-mate.

'Get off,' I mumbled, waking from a deep sleep. But the stroking continued and I was soon woken again, really angry this time and puzzled, too. We were generally very considerate of each other, and if we knew someone was in bed, tried to not disturb them. Almost more weary than when I had gone to bed, I traipsed down to the living room. 'Which one of you was touching my feet?' I asked. The other girls looked at me as if I was crazy. I went down the stairs, only to find our front door wide open. To this day I have no idea what happened that night.

The following evening was another university ball. We could never have afforded to go because the tickets were so expensive, but had planned, with military precision, to gatecrash after our late shifts had finished.

My housemates and I all decided to make our own dresses to save money. The event was black tie and there was no way I could have paid for a frock from one of Cambridge's best boutiques on my meagre nurse's salary. I had an old Singer sewing machine in my room and was quite handy with it, making all sorts of interesting ensembles. On that occasion, my creation was moss green, long and straight, with a lace overlay. I paired it with a flamboyant lilac boa I had found in a charity shop. To me, it was the perfect combination, although looking back, I am not so sure.

I had raced home after work and had only finished sewing at about 10 p.m., but I was delighted with my dress. Getting ready was all part of the fun and we gathered in the living room where we were joined by Marianne, Rashida, Cuth, Netty and Pondso, who brought along some wine for us to enjoy while we did our make-up.

At around 11 p.m. we raced through the cobbled streets, which echoed with the faint strains of jazz, our dresses hitched up around our ankles, and ran straight through one of the palatial college gates to join the party. By then everyone was so pie-eyed that no one asked us for our tickets and there was still plenty of delicious food and drink left. We couldn't believe our luck.

Our first stop was the buffet because we hadn't had time for dinner beforehand and were starving. We then danced the night away in one of the many tents – offering a choice of jazz, ballroom, country and jiving – spending half an hour at each in rotation, and chatted to the most handsome students we could see. Around 5 a.m., exhausted and exhilarated, we reluctantly returned home.

'I'm so hot,' I moaned, flinging my boa into a hedge on the way.

'Sue, you look like an exotic bird,' one of the other nurses exclaimed with a laugh. The lilac feathers had stuck to my skin and I left a trail across Cambridge as we walked along. By then I was too high on adrenalin to care.

At the end of my second year, I was told that I was to be transferred to a female ward in Chesterton old people's home and my heart sank. It was also some distance from our home in Bateman Street and I would have to leave for work earlier in the morning.

I arrived to find that the building was old and tired. As I climbed the stairs on my first morning, I noticed there were holes in the ragged carpet and that wallpaper was peeling from the walls in places. I hesitated at the entrance to the female ward, which smelt musty and of bodily fluids mixed with bleach. How depressing.

What had I come to?

At first there was no one around to tell me where I should leave my coat and bags, then a nurse greeted me and showed me to the locker room. The night nurse, a third-year student, gave us a report on all seventeen patients on the ward and told us what had happened during the night. Most of them had slept well, but the night nurse gave no diagnosis as to what was wrong with them, or what their social history was.

What was the matter with them? I wondered.

I spent the day changing beds stained with urine and faeces and helping the women on and off commodes, feeding those who were unable to feed themselves and noting all my actions on their charts. As the days passed, I slowly got to learn the ladies' names and often found myself wondering what was wrong with them, besides incontinence.

I sometimes felt that the dignity of the patients was not respected. I remember one very well-spoken lady whose husband had been a don at the university. She hated the routine of having to get up so early. This lady often used a commode and liked to be left alone for a while. One day I remember finding her, two hours later, very distressed because no one had come to help her off it. The curtain had not been properly pulled and she felt very exposed.

I also remember wondering why all the patients had to do everything at the same time, as there seemed to be far too much routine on the ward and not enough individual care. There was no entertainment that I can recall, only waiting for visitors, if the ladies were lucky. I felt that even though we were all busy, we were doing a job, and that it should be done properly. Even today this is one of the biggest complaints about care of the elderly – their dignity and respect is not always honoured.

I kept thinking of my grandmother and what she would have said. When I was really small, Mum, Dad and I lived with my grandmother who owned a lively public house, the Black Horse Inn in Telham, between Battle and Hastings. Her name was Maud Worsley but she was affectionately known by the pub regulars as 'The

Duchess' because she had a very regal air about her and would stand no nonsense. She appeared tall to me and was sturdy, with an ample bosom, a pale complexion, dark brown eyes and her thinning brunette hair always pulled into a firm bun. She was a widow – my grandfather had died before I was born. People used to say that I was just like my grandmother and my mum. 'You're good Worsley stock' they used to tell me.

As my mum had done when she was growing up, I would sit propped up in a corner, on a tall wooden stool in front of the bar, drinking my orange juice after school and chatting with the regulars, who always made a huge fuss of me. We had an open coal fire with red and orange flames licking the grate, so the pub was always warm and cosy. We served food and my grandmother seemed to be able to cook, serve at the bar and hold a conversation all at the same time. I remember that there was a constant supply of Walls vanilla and strawberry ice cream and sometimes, when I was really good, I was even allowed to help myself.

Later on, after I had qualified, my grandmother had a stroke and was admitted to her local hospital in Battle. I visited her with my mother several times and found it very upsetting – it was far too close for comfort. She was semi-conscious, confused and paralysed down one side, and I found myself withdrawing from her emotionally. I hate showing my emotions and at the time I felt I needed to be strong or else I would crumble. I found it difficult to talk about her condition without welling up. My mother and I helped bath her and one day I noticed that she had a pressure sore on her buttocks. When I asked the senior staff nurse how this had happened, she replied, 'It's because she cannot move on her own and they often get sore.' I didn't know what to say. I knew the nurses hadn't been turning her frequently enough, but I felt helpless. My biggest fear was that if I complained, the staff might take it out on my grandmother. She died about six weeks later and I hoped that she had not suffered. This episode certainly made me respect people when they are in need.

One lady, Gladys, in particular caught my attention. She had been at the home for ten years and couldn't walk very well. She usually looked miserable and had a terrible temper. She always smelt of what I think of as 'old ladies' body odour', lily of the valley mixed with stale urine. Her favourite word, it seemed, was no, particularly when it involved walking anywhere, and she was labelled 'lazy' by the staff. While I was working there, Gladys had no family visitors. I wondered whether she was bored and lonely. And had she really not been outside for ten years?

One sunny day, I asked the staff nurse if we could take Gladys out into the garden.

'It's impossible,' she told me. 'We can't get them down the stairs.'

'We could,' I replied, thinking on my feet. 'The porters could lift her in her wheelchair. It's quiet today. I'm sure they wouldn't mind.'

'Okay, if you can spare the time,' she said. 'But make sure that you have finished all your duties first.'

I bounded in to ask Gladys if she'd like to be taken down to the garden. My question was met with a grunt, so I took that as a yes.

I said I was going to give her a bed bath and some clean clothes. I'm sure she didn't believe I was really going to take her out until I washed her from top to bottom and covered her in talcum powder, then dressed her in a jumper and skirt and combed her thinning hair. I even put a spot of lipstick on her face. It took me a good hour to get her ready and presentable. Half an hour after that, the porters had deposited Gladys at the bottom of the stairs in her wheelchair.

Placing her walking aid in front of her and helping her slowly from the wheelchair, I was delighted to see that Gladys's face broke into a broad smile and, suddenly, she was off!

As I walked beside her, she kept saying, 'This is lovely. Look at the wonderful flowers; I can smell them. Are they roses I can see? How lovely! I can hear the birds singing.' It was a lovely spring day and the air was thick with the smell of cut grass.

It was as if the poor lady had been imprisoned and suddenly the world was open to her. Gladys was like a different woman and I vowed to myself that I would try and take her out again at least a few more times before I moved on from the Chesterton old people's home.

My third year started with a stint on the gynaecological ward at Addenbrooke's, the Goode Ward, and I was looking forward to having some interesting things to deal with after my time at the old people's home. One of the first patients I looked after was a middle-aged lady who was seriously ill with terminal breast cancer. She was very softly spoken and well-to-do. She told me she had taught at Girton College, the all-women's college in Cambridge, and loved it. Sadly, her tumour had fungated through the skin and produced a terrible odour. This poor lady always looked so clean and crisp in her cotton nightdresses, which only emphasised her delicate, bird-like appearance. She was terribly distressed by the smell of her wound, which penetrated the private room she occupied on the side of the ward. Nowadays, dressings impregnated with charcoal or some similar formula are used to control the stench. The lady insisted that we kept the window open and always had huge bunches of purple lavender in the room to help disguise it. Although we changed her dressing two or three times a day, the smell remained.

I often shared my worries with my flatmates, who went through similar experiences, and during the short time I was caring for this lady, I would find myself nursing a cup of coffee and talking about her.

'I feel so bad for her,' I said one night to Farida. 'She's so reluctant to have visitors. All she does is sit quietly reading her book when she's awake; it's so sad.'

'Poor lady, it sounds awful,' Farida replied.

'It's hard looking after elderly people,' I said. 'I feel so sorry for them sometimes. It's so undignified.'

'You're right. I don't ever want to get old and start losing my marbles. Hey, Sue, come on, cheer up and come out with me tonight. I'm meeting some Indian friends for a night of curry and music.'

I didn't feel like it, but I knew that a night out would help me forget about the poor lady in Goode Ward.

I remember the occasion well. Farida took me to her friend's house, where a group of women were cooking red and yellow curries and other delicious goodies. They were all dressed in colourful saris and the men more casual wear; some dressed in jackets and T-shirts. We all sat in a circle on cushions on the floor and the food was placed in the middle. The smell of musky joss sticks hung in the air, and listening to Ravi Shankar playing his sitar, and other Indian tunes, enhanced the authentic feel. I found the whining sound of women singing quite strange, not having come across many different cultures at that time. I was the only English person there, but everyone was very friendly, encouraging me to eat as much as possible.

On our way home, Farida linked her arm through mine. 'Forgotten about work?' she asked me.

'Work? What's that?' I said, knowing only too well that I would be back in the morning caring for the poor lady with the awful wound and filling vases with bunches of flowers. Whenever I smell lavender today, I still think of her.

But hospital life wasn't all sad – there was always plenty of laughter, too. After Goode Ward I went to the male surgical ward, Tipperary, also known as Nightingale because it was a large open room with about twenty-five beds. One of our tasks was to monitor the bowel movements of patients recovering from bowel surgery. One man was having trouble passing wind and was very uncomfortable, with some distension where his stomach was bloated. The doctor ordered an ox-bile enema for him. These are no longer used, but they were particularly good for treating wind. Nowadays, enemas are supplied in neat little plastic pouches, but back then they were administered with a jug of green soapy water or diluted ox bile, a glass funnel and a piece of red rubber tubing. We were told to give the fluid 'high, hot and a helluva lot'.

After pulling the curtains round the patient's bed I told him what I was going to do, asked him to turn on his right side and prepared the bed and equipment. I made sure I had a commode nearby, then I inserted the rubber tube, with the funnel attached, into his rectum and started to pour in the fluid. The height of the funnel determined the speed of the fluid going in; it was important to pour it in slowly so as not to irritate the bowel. If it went in too quickly, the patient might pass a large amount of fluid and nothing more. When we were still waiting after about twenty minutes, I helped the man on to the commode. We continued to wait but still nothing transpired, so I decided to return the equipment to the sluice. I was beginning to wonder what would happen to the poor man's swollen tummy if my intervention had not been effective. As I walked back to the ward I could hear someone cheering – the men were always looking out for one another or teasing each other. Just as I went behind the curtains, an explosive sound resonated round the ward with a loud echo. The enema had clearly been successful.

'It appears to be working, Nurse,' the patient said, emitting another squeak. I didn't know how much wind was still there, but there were several other thunderous bursts of activity and every time this happened there were roars and cheers from the men. The poor patient also started howling with laughter, which made matters worse. I was fighting the urge myself, but a small laugh escaped me. It is the little things in life that patients really appreciate. This one was forever grateful for that enema and made a speedy recovery.

All these experiences, and many more like them in the early days, helped me to learn and grow, both as a nurse and as a person. But the most challenging period of my nursing training was still to come – the children's ward.

The children's ward had long held the reputation among students of being the scariest and most difficult part of training. There was so much they hadn't encountered in other parts of their training and children became ill very, very fast. One bout of diarrhoea could mean life or death. I was frightened, too, but knew I was going to have to face my fears at some time, as two months' paediatrics was a compulsory part of my general training. It was towards the end of my third year at Addenbrooke's when I was told that the children's ward would be my final placement. I had never held a baby, except my brother, and was terrified I would drop one. Babies seemed so tiny and defenceless. I hoped it would not be the end of my career.

# 4

# The Children's Ward

As a child, I loved to bandage up my favourite rag doll. She had a permanent smile with candy-pink cheeks, long ginger pigtails and a blue spotted dress. I would listen to her heartbeat with my plastic stethoscope, then diagnose a broken arm or leg and bandage it accordingly with a piece of old rag which my mother would cut up for me.

Then, when I turned nine, my dream came true when my little brother, Peter, arrived. Having been an only child until then, I was thrilled to have my very own, living and breathing doll. He was eight weeks premature and only weighed two pounds, which was regarded as especially small in those days. My mother had been staying in hospital and my dad had gently warned me that Peter could die because he was so tiny. I prayed and prayed that he would be okay and constantly asked about him. When Mum eventually came home, Peter stayed in hospital until he had put on some more weight. Children in those days weren't allowed to visit, so when the day finally arrived for him to come home, it was such a big occasion that I was allowed to take the day off school. I was so excited I felt I could burst; it was better than my birthday and waking up on Christmas Day to see the overflowing red stocking at the end of my bed.

I waited in anticipation outside the ward while Mum

went in to collect Peter. It seemed to take ages and I was hopping from one foot to the other with impatience. Eventually, the nurse came out carrying him and she pulled back the top of the blanket to show me his face. I remember saying, 'Isn't he lovely!' but couldn't really see him properly for all the blankets he was wrapped in. We didn't have a car, so we travelled home on the bus and the journey seemed to take forever. When Peter was finally carried into the house, I could barely wait to have a proper look at him and I ordered Mum to strip off all his clothes. He was so small but quite perfect.

For the first few weeks Peter was at home, I would just stare in awe at his tiny rosebud mouth, button nose and sleeping eyes. I wanted him clean, comfortable and smelling sweetly, and would often help to bath him.

Mum was unable to breastfeed Peter for long, so he went on the bottle and I loved to feed him. I hated it if he cried; he would gasp for his next breath before letting out this high-pitched caterwaul. Despite his early appearance and small size, he caught up quickly, piled on the weight and soon turned into quite a bruiser, with a big chubby tummy and chunky arms and thighs. In his small beige duffel coat, he looked almost as wide as he was tall, like a human Paddington Bear.

As soon as Peter was big enough, I liked to use him as my patient. I would tie him to the tea trolley as tightly as I could manage and push him into the wall, sometimes numerous times in succession, and then nurse him better again. It sounds cruel now, but we would be laughing and fighting at the same time. If there was a real injury like a hard thump, there would be proper tears and Mum would shout at us to stop. We'd go quiet, at least for a few minutes, and then we would start up again. If anyone else was rough with Peter, even my father, I would be beside myself with anger. No one was allowed to hit my little brother, except me.

I remember another time, when my mum allowed me to take Peter for a walk in the pram. We had one of those magnificent, old-fashioned strollers with huge wheels. I don't know how, but Peter fell out and sustained a big yellow and blue bruise on his forehead. By the time we reached home it was as big as an egg and very angry-looking. I had heard that butter was good for bruises so, as soon as we got in, I rushed to the fridge, scooped out a handful and smeared it on his head, but it only seemed to make matters worse. Mum was furious with me and concerned about Peter, but by this time my little brother was his usual laughing self again. Thankfully, I was off the hook.

By the time I was working on Addenbrooke's paediatric ward, I knew that butter wouldn't do much for bruises, but I was learning rapidly about illnesses, especially childhood ones.

'Make sure you don't bash the children into the wall,' Peter would joke.

The paediatric ward was a mixed ward and treated children with medical conditions such as blood disorders, epilepsy and chest infections; also surgical problems such as appendicitis, hernias and other diagnoses. Most of the babies were ill with respiratory infections or gastroenteritis, especially during the winter months, the season for such illnesses.

On my first day on the ward I was overwhelmed by the noise – laughter, screaming, crying and clattering toys – it was so different from most other parts of the hospital. The ward always seemed to be busy and there were parents and siblings by most of the beds.

It also felt different from the other wards I had worked on. One of the biggest differences was that the children were dressed in colourful clothes, either their own or clothes provided by the hospital. All the adult patients I had nursed previously had only worn their own clothes when they went home. I would also learn that parents had a right to know all about their children's treatment, as we needed to work with the family. With adults, the situation was different; if a patient didn't want medical information given to their wife or husband, or any other family member, we had to respect their wishes.

Parents were often so stressed that they continuously asked questions, which could be very time-consuming. I often wondered how they coped with distressing news, and how they kept their families going, especially if they had other children. Some divided their time between visiting the hospital and looking after the child at home, while for others it was the mother who was the main visitor and the father would often visit in the evening after work. There was also the financial strain, especially if they were hard up; travelling to and from the hospital could expensive. It was rare for parents to stay overnight; this would only happen if a child was seriously ill, in which case we would erect a put-you-up by the patient's bed. However, this afforded little privacy and it was always cramped, especially if there was lots of equipment in the cubicle.

There were other differences. Children went to the hospital school if they were well enough. We used play as a tool to help explain to them about their operations and treatments. The drug doses were much smaller and calculated differently, according to the child's weight, rather than their age, as with adults. Whereas most adult drugs were in the form of tablets, all the children's medicines were in liquid form, which made them easier to administer. Even so, young patients were sometimes more reluctant than adults to take their medicine. Sometimes we mixed them with jam or some other sweetener to try and disguise the flavour.

There were many diseases I had not heard of before. In my first week on the children's ward, I remember being shocked when a baby boy was brought in suffering from suspected pyloric stenosis. I had no idea what this was, but soon learnt that it was the narrowing of the pylorus, the lower part of the stomach through which food and other digested matter passes to enter the small intestine. When an infant has pyloric stenosis, the muscles in the pylorus have become enlarged and cause a narrowing within the pyloric channel, to the point where food is prevented from leaving the stomach. This little boy was projectile vomiting milk all over the place, especially when he was being fed. His poor mother was at her wits' end and he was at risk of becoming dehydrated due to salt and fluid imbalance. To diagnose the problem, the doctor bandaged the baby's arms to a wooden crucifix. He was crying inconsolably at first, but soon rested in his mother's arms and was given a feed with a bottle. The doctor then palpated his abdomen to see if a tumour or hard lump could be felt. Luckily, he stood to the side, because the baby vomited everywhere as the doctor pushed his little tummy down. I could even see the waves across his stomach where the muscles were trying to move the food along. It was confirmed that this was the problem and, after surgery, the little boy was cured and happily soon able to go home.

Among the other unusual diseases I encountered on the paediatric ward were congenital heart disease, cleft lip and palate – then known as hair lip and palate – oesophageal fistular and atresia, where the food pipe was not open or there was a hole in the windpipe, with the consequent risk of choking if fed, and anal atresia where the opening to the anus was missing or blocked.

My eight weeks in paediatrics were certainly challenging. As the people suggested, it was more difficult than other parts of the training, and also different. Taking the blood pressure of babies was hard because they were usually screaming and squirming; finding veins before a blood test was horrible; and worst of all was the irrational fear that I had of babies choking, especially those with respiratory problems. I was terrified that, when feeding them to see if they could suckle, they would choke to death because their airways were so small. I learnt that a major difference between children and adults is that it is more common for babies to suffer from respiratory arrest before cardiac arrest, whereas cardiac arrests are more likely to occur first in adults. Because of this, basic resuscitation involves a slightly different ratio of breaths to chest compressions, with five initial breaths to help pump oxygen into the lungs, before chest compressions. I was constantly worried that I would miss something important.

Most of the children were in and out of hospital within a few days and often there were from fifteen to twenty admissions a day, so I didn't get to know any of them particularly well. However, I did know that I had to form a good relationship with the child very quickly; if they didn't like you, you were ruined! I saw that life was mostly black and white to them. If you were gentle and kind, and explained everything carefully in a language they could understand, however basic – including that teddy was having the treatment, too – it worked, most of the time. I made a point of never looking over the child's head to the parents, but always including the patient when talking through treatment. I even tried to talk to small babies; it's quite amusing how they will respond, as if they are having a conversation with you.

Such was the high turnover in the paediatric ward that there was a 'black book' in which were recorded the name, age and weight of each child admitted, details of what they were being treated for and the treatment required, so that nothing was overlooked.

Although the ward was very busy, the sister in charge always knew what was going on. Several groups of doctors would often be on the ward at the same time, such as the general surgeons, the ENT (ear, nose and throat) surgeons and haematology doctors, and they would all have to report to the head nurse. Each nurse had patients allocated to her according to her experience and seniority, or how ill the children were. I always dreaded being asked to keep an eye on things while the staff nurse was in theatre. I was worried I would be unsure of what to do in the event of a crisis, but I always coped, despite my panic.

At the end of our shifts we would do a handover around Sister's desk, when everything was reported, and because this was always very detailed, it could sometimes take up to an hour. She would tell us the name, age and diagnosis of each child, report on their condition and any change in treatment, and any tests or operations they were to have. If it was a morning shift, someone was allocated the milk room, where enough baby feeds were made up in glass bottles to last for twenty-four hours. No feed was kept longer than that and there was a strict routine of hygiene: you wore a long white gown, mask and cap and no one could enter the room while feeds were being made up. Metal bowls had to be sterilised by boiling, so it was a full-time job. And you had to finish by lunchtime, otherwise you missed out on lunch.

The senior nurse, who would do the medicine rounds at 6 a.m., 10.a.m., noon, 2 p.m., 6 p.m., 10 p.m. and midnight, would be responsible for the drug keys. Only very occasionally were drugs dispensed at 2 a.m. The senior nurse and another nurse would go round the ward with the medicine trolley and the prescription charts. If there were injections to be given, these would be done last and prepared in the treatment room, out of sight of the children. We always gave injections with two nurses – one to hold and comfort the child and the other to give the drug. If the mother was willing, we would show her how to hold the child firmly, especially if the child was having long-term treatment.

Before we went off duty in the evening – more often than not well past 10 p.m. – we had to ensure that the various colourful plastic and wooden toys were put away and the ward was tidy. Sometimes, after a particularly busy day, we were still doing the 6 p.m. drugs round when the night nurses came on duty at 8.30 p.m. There was a real spirit of teamwork on the ward. If a nurse rang in sick, we would stay on until the work was done. Even the night sister would sometimes help out with the drugs round if she wasn't too busy.

When I first started on the children's ward, I was afraid to answer some of the anxious parents' questions in case I gave them wrong information, but I gradually gained confidence and knew when to refer them to the more senior nurses or doctors. I enjoyed the parents' company, getting to know the different families and trying to allay their anxieties. I took pleasure in carefully explaining diagnoses and treatments to them, so that they understood what was wrong with their children, and they were always grateful. I soon learnt that if you kept them informed and were strictly honest with them, they appreciated it. I made sure I never skirted around the facts. Later in my career I enjoyed teaching and I guess this was the start of that.

One child I looked after while I was on night duty at that time was a girl by the name of Rebecca. She was a sweet, ginger-haired child of eight and was suffering from leukaemia from which, sadly, at that time, the majority of children who had the illness died. The treatment has advanced so much since then that nowadays 90 per cent will be cured. However, Rebecca's prognosis wasn't favourable. I was fast learning that sometimes it was harder looking after older children than it was caring for the smaller ones because they understood more, and Rebecca knew she was desperately ill. She had been in and out of hospital for months and was having some more blood platelets intravenously because her blood count was low. These days they would be given routinely, but back then we would wait for the patient's blood count to drop before giving them.

Rebecca had struggled to go to sleep that night and was tearful and anxious. The visiting hours for parents were strict, so her mother had gone home hours before. After a cuddle, I had read her one of her favourite stories by Enid Blyton, in an attempt to calm her down, and eventually she had dropped off and was sleeping soundly.

Then, at 2 a.m., she woke up and vomited.

'I'm dying, I'm dying,' she yelped, in floods of tears. 'I'm bleeding to death.'

I looked down and her vomit was deep red and mottled. I tried desperately to reassure her because I knew that anxiety could increase the bleeding – a complication of the disease and her low platelets. I didn't know exactly how ill she was or her blood count, because I was still learning about illnesses. I knew how to nurse her, but if she haemorrhaged I would have no idea what to do. I would have to call the night sister, who would call the doctor if necessary. Much of what I was learning then was nursing by numbers – following steps one, two and three. I knew nothing about the complexities of children's illnesses.

'I know it looks a lot but it's just a little bit of blood mixed with all the food you've eaten and everything you've drunk. You are not dying now, sweetheart,' I told her, trying not to sound nervous. 'It'll be fine. Just relax. You're just feeling a bit poorly. You'll feel better if you're calm. Don't cry.'

I brought her close to me and stroked her back. Her breathing started to slow down and her hunched shoulders relaxed.

'Is Mum coming tomorrow?'

'Yes, she is, she'll be here in just a few hours,' I told her. 'If you shut your eyes now, she'll be here before you know it.'

'Will you stay with me?'

'Yes, I will. Why don't I read you some more from *Malory Towers*? That will take your mind off it.'

As I read, slowly and calmly, about Darrell Rivers' latest adventures, her eyes started to close and she drifted off to sleep again. I secretly wished I could cure all these children, but knew it was not possible. I longed to be the warm, comforting presence that children craved.

As Rebecca drifted off, my mind wandered back to an experience I had when I was about six. I was outside, in the garden of my grandmother's pub. It was a wintry Sunday afternoon and I couldn't wait to jump in the big puddles in my new bright yellow wellies. We had a wiry German gardener who was a former prisoner of war. He was always working hard to make sure the outside of the pub looked welcoming, and on that particular day he had been raking up the last of the leaves. As I ran through the grass blindly, I careened straight into the rake and toppled awkwardly on to my elbow. I screamed and wailed and nothing could stop my tears. Mum rushed me straight to the local hospital, but we were packed off home again and told to come back the next day, when the X-ray room would be open. That night was agony. I couldn't sleep and was inconsolable. My arm was all floppy and it was so painful. I hated the sensation of being unable to move my fingers properly, and a new wave of pain crashed over me every time I tried. Mum did her best to comfort me, stroking my hair and cuddling me, but nothing worked.

Arriving back at the hospital the following day, we were greeted by a stout-looking lady with thickset eyebrows and greying hair. She reminded me of a wise owl. Seeing my tear-stained face, she enveloped me in her larger-than-average bosom. 'There, there,' she cooed. 'We'll set you right in no time. I think I have jelly babies for special girls. And if you're really good, I might have an animal sticker somewhere.'

Mum looked on gratefully. Suddenly everything looked marginally rosier and I went off to be X-rayed. Later, after a fracture had been diagnosed, the kindly nurse held my hand and kept talking to me, while the doctor applied a white plaster cast over my bent arm. Afterwards she gently put it into a sling.

'What a brave girl,' she said with a smile, attaching the sticker to my sling. 'All the other girls will want one of these now.' I couldn't stop smiling.

I felt frustrated that I did not know enough about Rebecca's illness and the impact it had on her family. How long would she live? Was there anything else I could do to help her? But I rationalised that I couldn't know or do everything. What little I was doing was a small thing in this child's life, but I hoped it helped, like the nurse who had helped my mother and me that day.

Despite my initial apprehension about nursing children and babies on the children's ward, I grew to love looking after them. Once my fears had diminished I thrived on the learning process; it seemed that I was gathering more knowledge every day. I would wake up excited about what the day might bring. I was in my element. I loved making the children smile and the way they found happiness in the most simple things. There was never any side to any of them. It was incredibly rewarding.

I also got to know one of my great friends, Cuth, on the children's ward. We had socialised together because she lived in the nurses' flat in nearby Marshall Road, but I had never worked with her. She was three months ahead of me and helped me a lot in my first few weeks, showing me the ropes.

I knew I had made the grade with Sister Hucknall when, during my last week, I was cleaning out the baby sluice and unintentionally making a lot of noise, clattering the metal potties and buckets around.

'Who is making all the noise?' she shouted.

I looked up from the hard floor where I was on my hands and knees trying to organise the potties.

'I might've known it was you, Nurse Macqueen!'

I'm sure I saw a twinkle in her eye.

After passing my third-year exams and qualifying, I initially felt on top of the world. We celebrated the results with an evening of drinking and dancing. I felt like I had finally made it. However, I soon arrived back down to earth with a bump, when the realisation hit me that this was just the beginning of learning what a huge responsibility it was to be a nurse.

It felt natural to apply for a staff nurse job on the children's ward at Addenbrooke's and my wish was granted. That did not happen to all the nurses, so I was delighted that I had landed my first 'proper job'. However, the first time I put on my new square cap and purple belt with the silver buckle that my mother had bought me, I felt totally inadequate. I felt I was expected to know everything, be responsible for everything, and yet my knowledge was still limited.

There was a high turnover of children coming into the ward, some only staying for short periods of time, and this made it difficult to form relationships. From time to time, however, the same children would be readmitted for longer periods. As time passed, my confidence grew and there was always someone to ask if I didn't know the answers.

One of the first little faces I recognised as I took up my staff nurse post was Hannah's. Aged three, she had cystic fibrosis, a genetic disorder affecting the internal organs, especially the lungs and digestive system, by clogging them with a thick, sticky mucus. Hannah was in and out of hospital for treatment and monitoring.

She was back with us because she had yet another chest infection. It was long before the days when cystic fibrosis sufferers received effective treatment: now they are offered lung transplants and so can lead relatively normal lives. In those days the prognosis wasn't great and, sadly, Hannah wasn't expected to live into her teenage years. However, she had an incredible amount of energy for a girl who was so small and skinny and would never, ever, stop talking in her high-pitched voice.

She noticed everything that went on around her and asked constant questions: 'What are you doing?' 'Why have you got a syringe?' 'Who is the girl in that bed?'

Hannah had a remarkable vocabulary for a three-year-old, especially when it came to medical things – a clear indicator of the time she spent on the ward, soaking up the world around her like a sponge.

She had to have four-hourly antibiotic injections and lots of medicines, and sometimes required oxygen. She also needed medication to aid her digestion. She hated her injections and knew exactly what was happening. She would constantly tell us: 'Teddy doesn't want it so I don't want it. Teddy says no-thank-you.'

On other occasions she would cry and beg us not to do them, although she understood that she had to have the injections to make her well. All the nurses hated giving them to her – she would cry and squirm – and we always made a point of cuddling her at the same time.

Hannah also needed four-hourly physiotherapy on her chest. We would put her on top of a pillow with her head down and, cupping our hands on her chest, spend fifteen minutes on each side, patting away to try and release some mucus. She would then get terrific bouts of coughing which would make her go red and blue in the face. The physiotherapy would leave her exhausted and sweating, and was often quite breathless herself. Hannah was salty to kiss and smelt metallic, an effect of the medicine she took, called Pancrex, for her digestion. She was great fun, though, and always brightened our days when she was in a good mood and happy.

One evening when I was on night duty, I was exhausted. We worked long hours: the shifts ran from 8.30 p.m. until 8 a.m. the following morning and operated on a rotating basis. I found that adjusting my body clock still hadn't got any easier. It was especially hard to sleep in the daytime and I always woke mid-afternoon when my flatmates came home, however much they tiptoed around trying not to disturb me.

That day I hadn't managed much sleep, as there had been a cacophony of drilling from the road works in progress outside the house. In fact, I'd only had a couple of hours' sleep, and after lying awake tossing and turning for another hour or so, I'd given up.

It must have been about 2 a.m. and I was so tired my eyes prickled and felt like lead. Everything was quiet on the ward as the children slept; the only sound was the odd snuffle. I decided to put my head down on the nurses' desk – not a very comfortable place to sleep but I just wanted to rest for five minutes.

After what seemed like only a few moments of blissful relaxation, although it may have been more like ten minutes, I heaved myself up and returned to work – taking observations, feeding the children through tubes, checking drips and doing medications.

As I neared the front of the ward, a little voice piped up, 'I saw you asleep.'

Hannah – I should have known. I looked over and saw that she was sitting on her pillow against the bars of the bed.

'Me? Asleep. No – I was just doing some notes about the other children ...'

'No. I saw you. You were asleep and I am going to tell Sister.' She giggled.

'Anyway, why are we talking about me sleeping? You're the one that's supposed to be asleep! It's the middle of the night.'

She giggled again. 'I *am* going to tell Sister.'

I felt slightly nervous; surely Sister wouldn't believe her? It's a disciplinary offence these days to fall asleep on the job. Back then, I knew I shouldn't have done it and Sister was strict. In the morning, however, we laughed it off and nothing more was said. I was very relieved indeed.

Hannah was such a fun kid to have on the ward that when her fourth birthday approached a couple of weeks later, we made plans to give her a special party.

Her mother had come in early and dressed her in a pretty pink dress with fairy wings; like most young girls of that age, Hannah loved all things pink.

'I look like a princess,' she announced.

We tried as hard as we could to vary her time while she was with us, so that it didn't seem like a constant round of injections and physiotherapy. We would often be forced to stop her doing her latest drawing or interrupt her play because of her treatments.

On the day of the party, we timed it so that Hannah had taken all her medications and had a good few hours before her next lot of injections and physio.

'It's time,' I said. 'We're having a party!'

'For me?' Her eyes shone and she started rasping with excitement.

All the nurses, the other children, some doctors, Hannah and her mum gathered round the bed of a boy who was on traction because of a broken leg.

We set up a table with nibbles and drinks – orange squash, salt and vinegar crisps and little cheese sandwiches.

Hannah was beside herself with excitement, laughing and coughing and trying to speak all at the same time.

'And this is for you!' I handed her a carefully wrapped present with a bow on top. She ripped into it, throwing aside the paper as she did so and pulled out the dolly inside by its yellow hair.

'I love it!' she exclaimed, kissing the doll on the lips and stroking down her dress and coughing some more. 'Dolly says today is a good day!'

Then it was time for some cake – it was pink with flowers and four candles – and everyone broke into a tuneless round of 'Happy Birthday'.

Hannah giggled and breathlessly blew out her candles, coughing all over the cake in the process. We duly tucked into it, trying not to think about the mucus, and everyone was happy. It almost felt as if we were in a village hall somewhere in the country. Before long, though, it was back to work – and back to more injections.

As the ward was on the ground floor, the children could play in the small garden outside. There was a little blue slide and a red and yellow Noddy-type car, along with a sandpit and bucket and spades. In the summer, we would sometimes put out the paddling pool, which was a real favourite with the children. The beds would be wheeled outside if it was warm enough and sometimes the children ran about and shrieked so much you could be forgiven for wondering why they were in hospital at all. Hannah loved the slide and would spend all day on it, going up the little steps and gliding down again with a loud 'weeeee' and a cough for good measure. Of course someone had to supervise these activities, as there were sometimes tears if the children tripped or didn't want to share. This could be difficult if we were very busy on the ward, but the parents were always happy to help.

When I heard, a few years later, that Hannah had passed away, I felt for her poor parents. My flatmate Cuth later told me that she often saw the mother and father around town, as she continued to work in Cambridge as a health visitor, She said they would always stop and talk. They seemed to have coped with the situation very well and appreciated how much we had all loved Hannah.

After a year in the job, I decided that it was no good looking after all these children if I didn't understand the basics of how they were born. So off I went to Southmead Hospital in Bristol, to do my Midwifery Part 1, as it was then called.

I enjoyed living in Bristol and visiting places like Wookey Hole, but I didn't particularly enjoy the work. The majority of the pregnant women were always moaning about their swollen ankles, tiredness, back-ache, indigestion, cravings and nausea; some days it felt like a never-ending list of complaints. As far as I was concerned, these women were just pregnant, not ill, and after some mothers had given birth, I felt frustrated when they expected us to do everything for them, from putting the child to their breast to feed, to changing their babies' nappies and cleaning up after them in the bathrooms. It was a different matter if they had had a Caesarean section, but I felt that some ladies treated the hospital like a hotel. Women then routinely stayed for up to ten days, sometimes longer, regardless of the type of delivery they had had. Many of them used the time to have a good rest, while we rushed about cleaning, tidying and organising them. Antenatal care felt tame by comparison with the work I had been doing. Some of the people I was training with loved it, but it wasn't for me.

However, I did enjoy looking after the ill patients, such as those with pre-eclampsia. This is a disease where the blood vessels constrict for some reason, caus-ing high blood pressure, known as hypertension, and renal, liver and brain damage. It affected about ten per cent of pregnant women at that time. Symptoms include oedema, where the patient has swollen legs, feet and hands, and high levels of protein in the urine. Although I knew the theory of the seriousness of the illness, I only looked after one patient who was very ill with eclamp-sia: a girl called Claire, in her mid-twenties, who about six months into her first pregnancy. She was in a coma after a seizure and needed constant care. Tragically, she lost her baby, but slowly started to recover afterwards, which is more often than not the case with eclampsia patients. This seemed amazing to me. Obviously I had a lot to learn.

It was important that the area in which Claire was nursed was quiet, as any sudden noise could bring on another fit. Her cubicle was kept dark and she was heavily sedated. We had to take her blood pressure every half-hour and she was given drugs to bring it down, as there was a real risk of a brain haemorrhage, leading to brain damage. She was turned every two hours to prevent chest infections and pressure sores, and was given a bed bath every day. She had a urinary catheter inserted so we were able to measure her urine output and also test her urine – it was important to monitor the albumen content, as the presence of large amounts could be a sign of malfunctioning kidneys. It was only after losing the baby that this slowly started to fall.

Claire's husband, a mild-mannered man, was constantly at her bedside. He seemed to get thinner, and his hair appeared greyer by the day, as he sat holding her hand and fighting sleep. Whenever I tried to make him take a break, he was insistent that he wanted to stay by her side.

Claire's mother also visited, bringing fresh nighties, and on the rare occasions when she managed to persuade her son-in-law to go home, she would sit and talk quietly to Claire, even though always tearful and anxious.

'The little one was going to be my fifth grandchild,' she said. 'I had already started knitting bootees. And now, look at her, poor Claire, my poor darling. It seems like yesterday that she was a baby herself . . .'

Claire was left with permanent kidney damage and I do not know if the couple went on to have another child because we lost contact. She was young so I'm hopeful that they did.

Despite my reservations about antenatal care, I did enjoy the exciting birth process and looking after the newborns, who were, without exception, delightful. The babies were always taken away from the mothers at night to help them rest and recover from the birth, so there was plenty of screaming from the nursery. They would be lined up in rows of cots, swaddled in cellular white blankets, like a file of small human cocoons. The only way of telling them apart, other than by looking at the different features of their tiny faces, was by the plastic name tags dangling from their miniature ankles; pink ones for girls and blue for boys. Having to look after as many as thirty-five babies at times, and feed them every three to four hours, with only five or six of us on duty, sometimes felt like being on a treadmill. It was like a military operation, but I quickly learnt how to feed two babies at a time, not by propping up a bottle in the cot, as that was forbidden, but by holding one wriggling newborn in each arm. It was very, very rarely quiet in the nursery, as one baby would start crying and it would set them all off in high-pitched unison. If one of us dropped something on the floor with a clatter, the crying would start up all over again. The other nurses, midwives and I always had plenty to talk about and supported one another if things got busy during the early hours of the morning.

During our six months' midwifery training, we had to deliver ten normal births, as well as witness a number of abnormal births, such as breech delivery, where the baby is born feet first, attend Caesarean sections and perform a number of vaginal examinations. Some students were even lucky enough to see twins being born. They are far more common now than they were then, due to the advent of fertility treatment.

My first delivery took place on one occasion while I was on night duty, a couple of months into my training. By then I had assisted the Southmead midwives in many births, but had never actually had the experience of delivering a baby myself. It had been a hectic night and there had already been two or three babies born on the ward.

The lady I was looking after was in her early thirties, which was older than a lot of the young mothers we saw at that time. I was incredibly tense, but tried not to show it, as she pushed and panted and shouted angrily, with her legs in leather stirrups. I was determined to see this one through, even though my shift was nearly over. She knew I was going to stay for the birth and we struck up a good relationship.

'Do you know I'm just sitting here staring at your bum?' I told the mother, trying to make her laugh as I gazed intently at her purple perineum, waiting for something to happen. She had had some pain relief – a pethidine injection in her thigh – and between painful contractions was quite jolly, chatting about her two younger children who were at home with their Nana.

'Hurry up, I'm getting sick of the sight of it,' I told her.

'Oh piss off,' she shouted back, laughing and wincing, as she felt another intense wave of pain coming on.

At the time, it was a routine procedure to do episiotomies to prevent women from tearing because they are easier and cleaner to stitch up. So, gowned up with sterile gloves and with a trolley containing the necessary instruments, I took the sterile scissors and prepared for my first episiotomy. As I made the angular incision during a contraction, the skin felt tough, like cutting a joint of well-done meat. I thought I had made a huge cut but when the contraction eased it was far smaller than it had felt – thank goodness. At the next contraction I tried again and this time the cut was longer and more satisfactory, according to the midwife supervising me. I was terrified the baby would slip through my hands, like a fish, and end up on the hard floor, but when the head finally crowned, the delivery was like clockwork. After the head came out, I twisted the shoulders, eased the upper shoulder out, then the lower one, and the baby slid into my hands. He had a shock of dark hair. I laid him, bloody and damp, on his mother's stomach.

'Oh he's so beautiful,' she cried.

I felt the cord and waited for it to stop pulsating, then clamped it to stop any bleeding. Then I cut the cord above the clamp and wrapped the baby up in a towel and gave him to his mum, before delivering the placenta. After weighing and measuring him, I gave him back to her. It was an incredible feeling, I felt on top of the world.

After doing the normal checks and making sure that both mother and baby were clean, I went to find the father who had been waiting in the visitors' room. Back in those days, men never attended the delivery but always remained in another room – or the pub! The midwife had told him immediately after the birth that he had a baby boy and he couldn't wait to see him. The excitement filled the air and I felt really privileged to be part of it. I thought how wonderful nature was. You cannot describe the love for a child but you can feel it; it's as if the air around you warms up and you can see an invisible ribbon from the heart of the mother to that of her child. It's a wonderful feeling and it never diminished throughout my career.

Although I loved babies and children, I was not very broody for my own. I know it may sound strange, but even though I would eagerly cuddle my friends' babies, I was only too happy to hand them back again. I never did have children of my own and never regretted it. I was so busy pursuing my career that the time never seemed right for it.

After I felt I had grasped the basics of newborns and delivering babies, I was more than happy to return to my staff nurse post at Addenbrooke's. I remembered how I had felt when I was training and vowed to be kind, patient, understanding and supportive to the more junior nurses when I came back. I was not so aware of what was going on in the rest of the hospital; I could only concentrate on my role on the children's ward and the responsibilities that entailed.

Back in Cambridge, I moved into a lovely house with Cuth and two other nurses, Pat and Margaret. Now that we were trained and earning a little more money, we found ourselves a more respectable abode to rent in Willow Walk. We felt very upmarket indeed and loved throwing dinner parties there for all our friends, with plenty of wine to distract our guests on those occasions when our dishes hadn't quite gone to plan. Margaret had been living at home while we were in Bristol doing midwifery, but had managed to get a job at Addenbrooke's on Thomas Potter Ward. We were later joined by Ruth, who was a friend of Margaret's in Bristol, an attractive, sensual girl with fair hair. Ruth had been about to get married, but got cold feet and walked away on the day of the wedding. Naturally, there was a lot of distress in both families and the returning of toasters, towels, and so on. Her mother took the wedding cake to a fete where people were invited to guess its weight. When Ruth was asked, she replied, 'It's like a millstone!' She was great fun and a fantastic cook, and always had plenty of boyfriends around her; I think she had taken on a new lease of life after her narrow escape. Although she was not a nurse, she was the perfect fifth person in our little nurses' family.

I remember having my one and only bout of flu while I was living in Willow Walk. I was always healthy and only had a few days' sick leave in a career that spanned fifty-odd years. I seem to be blessed with a robust constitution, which is just as well working in a hospital. On this occasion, I was off work for seven days and felt absolutely terrible. I had a soaring temperature and aching limbs that seemed to be glued to the mattress whenever I tried to move. When I finally managed to get out of bed to go to the toilet, I felt faint and would have to lie down on the bathroom floor, before making the arduous journey back to my bedroom. I was also constantly cold, shivering so hard that my teeth chattered, even when I had piled every warm cover I could find on to my bed. I couldn't stop crying and after one of my worried flatmates called my mother, she came over with oranges and flu remedies. She offered to look after me at home, but I was adamant that I wanted to stay at Willow Walk. Mum only agreed when Cuth and Ruth said they would look in on me as often as they possibly could and bring me anything I needed.

One day Ruth came in from work and rushed upstairs to see me. I had been drifting in and out of sleep and was very dazed.

'Sue, this room smells really strongly of gas,' she said. 'It's seriously bad.'

She walked over to the dingy gas fire. It had been on most of the time I had been ill, to try and warm up the room.

'Is this fire supposed to be on? There's no flame.'

'I put it on this morning. Or I think I did.'

She dashed out of the room and reappeared ten minutes later.

'There are workmen outside doing something in the road, but they said they had turned the gas supply back on again. Sorry, I'm going to have to open all the windows to let these fumes out.'

It only occurred to me later, when I was starting to feel better, what I narrow escape I had had. If the windows hadn't been letting in fresh air and letting out the fumes before Ruth's arrival, I might not have lived to tell the tale.

One of my colleagues at Addenbrooke's at that time was called Annie, a statuesque girl with bright red curly hair and porcelain skin. The other nurses had nicknamed her 'Alligator Annie' because all the doctors fancied her and she liked to flirt. None of us stood a chance with any of the men while Annie was around. There was a particularly good-looking houseman, a tall Chinese man by the name of Dr Chung, with a sharp jaw and bulging biceps. We all adored him and would race to help him at every opportunity when he came on the ward. However, much to our distress, it was pretty clear that Dr Chung's favourite nurse was Annie.

Not only that. More importantly, in my eyes, Annie had done her three years' training at Great Ormond Street, before doing more general paediatrics at

Addenbrooke's. Because of this, she had a much better knowledge of children's diseases than I did, especially the more rare conditions that were common at GOSH. The 'pink nurses' were loved by everyone and I felt they were seen as being in a league of their own, both by the patients and by the more senior staff. Even though we were on the same level, I noticed that the doctors often referred to Annie rather than me, which was extremely frustrating. One night, when we were on duty together, we had an emergency call from the paediatrician, Dr Gairdner. A baby had been born on the maternity unit with respiratory distress which might be due to a congenital abnormality.

'We need to get the cubicle ready,' she said. I had no idea where to start.

'We need to heat the incubator, get the resuscitation trolley, call the anaesthetist and ask him to bring a baby ventilator,' she ordered.

Not long afterwards, Dr Gairdner came in with the baby from the maternity unit and the baby's anxious father. Annie and I took the baby, a little girl, estimated her weight and got her settled. She was put on a ventilator, and then Annie and the doctor took her to be X-rayed. It was later confirmed that this *was* a case of tracheoesophageal fistula and atresia, where the food pipe is not patent and there is a hole between the food and windpipe, which can cause severe chest infections, and we arranged for the baby to be transferred to GOSH for surgery. I remember the registrar who made the telephone call to the hospital being very nervous, and making sure he had all the necessary notes and X-rays to hand, in case he was questioned. Nowadays, X-rays and medical notes are sent electronically, and maintaining confidentiality, so the immediate detailed care of the patient can be discussed over the phone.

After my shift, I had time to think about what had happened and, it was crystal clear to me that I must go to GOSH for further training, so that I could acquire more of the specialist knowledge I would need to be the best children's nurse I possibly could.

# 5

# My Early Weeks at GOSH

The Hospital for Sick Children in Great Ormond Street (which was officially renamed Great Ormond Street Hospital for Children in 1994) originally opened its doors on St Valentine's Day, 14 February 1852. Founded by the dynamic Dr Charles West, one of its earliest champions was the author Charles Dickens, who loved children and called them 'fresh from God'. It was the first hospital in England to treat children; at the time, even the large London hospitals didn't have separate children's wards and only a very small number of them dealt with children. Rickets, tuberculosis and malnutrition were rife and only half of those born reached adulthood. The hospital, located at No. 49, Great Ormond Street, opened with little ceremony. It had just two ten-bedded wards, one for girls and one for boys, and two doctors, Dr West and Dr William Jenner. The number of beds would triple by the end of its first year. Its aims were to provide medical treatment for the children of the poor during sickness, promote the advancement of medical science, and to be available to all classes of the community.

The new hospital also aimed to employ and train women specifically in children's nursing. Dr West recognised that the job of the nurse was critical to the success of his hospital, but the majority of doctors viewed nurses as servants, who could provide patients with clean clothes and good food. However, rather than the nurses being managed by physicians, an unpaid lady superintendent was now employed to supervise them. But reports on the quality of nursing at the time seemed to suggest that there were plenty of shortcomings.

The hospital's first patient was a three-and-a-half-year-old, Eliza Armstrong, whose family was too poor to pay for treatment. She had consumption, the non-medical word for tuberculosis, a common and often fatal disease in those days. Medicine was very different then. Cures were in short supply and, as a result, Eliza was admitted as an inpatient and given rest and good meals, including milk, beef tea and even wine. She left three weeks later, to attend as an outpatient. The first outpatient was two-year-old George Parr, who was suffering from catarrh and diarrhoea. Great Ormond Street Hospital was regarded with suspicion at first, but after a few months the number of patients gradually increased and the hospital itself grew in size, purchasing the neighbouring house, No. 48, in 1858, and opening the first purpose-built building in 1875.

The post of unpaid lady superintendent was created in 1862. The most famous of these was Catherine Wood, who wrote a number of books and was feared by many. She worked without payment for the hospital for almost twenty-five years, between 1863 and 1888, and is said to have laid the foundations for modern paediatric nursing and training.

Since its formation, the hospital's goals have been to find new and better ways to treat childhood illnesses. From its earliest days, it was always the place where the most distinguished doctors and specialists transformed children's lives for the better.

The hospital is famous for two things: making sick children better and being the second home of Peter Pan. I already knew the connection with Peter Pan and J. M. Barrie. Although he and his wife had no children, Barrie loved young people and supported GOSH for many years. In 1929, he was approached to sit on a committee to help buy some land so that the hospital could build a new wing. He declined to serve on the committee, but said he hoped to find another way to help. Two months later, he gifted the rights of *Peter Pan* to the hospital, which was a remarkable act of generosity. His only request was that the amount of money raised should never be disclosed. At a dinner which Barrie hosted later that year, he claimed that Peter had been a patient at GOSH and 'It was he who put me up to the little thing I did for the hospital.'

Since then, every time a book is sold or a production of *Peter Pan* put on, the hospital receives a royalty. Barrie was a big supporter of GOSH and my first ward, the cardiac ward, was on the Barrie Wing, named after him in recognition of his gift of the rights to his most famous work. The story of Peter, Wendy, Tinkerbell and the Lost Boys was one of my favourites as a child.

After my initial stint on the cardiac ward looking after Henry, the eight-year-old with a hole in the heart, I nursed some other babies and gradually started to feel less nervous and more like one of the team. For my next assignment, I was sent for two months to the observation ward at a hospital in Hackney, the Queen Elizabeth

Hospital for Children. It was jointly managed by Great Ormond Street in a grand old Victorian building with just over a hundred beds. It was very dilapidated and rundown, but much loved by the local East End population. The observation ward had ten cubicles and many of the children were ill with gastroenteritis. The sister, Sister Richards, was an old dragon and as I was one of the first 'strings' to be sent there, I would often come under fire. It didn't take me long to discover that the staff resented the GOSH nurses, who were thought to be snooty. This was the first time I had felt unsupported and even picked on by my superiors and fellow nurses.

Sister Richards would always be asking me questions to test my knowledge and I felt she was undermining me all the time. Once I had to pass a naso-gastric tube into the stomach of a baby with gastroenteritis. I proceeded to pass the tube and got it into the stomach at the first attempt. There is a risk that the tube will go into the lungs but I could feel by touch that it had gone down smoothly.

'How many inches has it gone down?' Sister Richards asked in a huffy voice.

'I haven't measured it but I know it's fine,' I replied as diplomatically as I could, as I had done this procedure hundreds of times before.

'No, do it again,' she instructed.

Poor child, I thought.

'But it is in the stomach. Look, I have aspirated the stomach contents and the blue litmus paper has turned pink.' This was confirmation that it was in the correct position.

'Stop arguing with me, Nurse Macqueen, and re-pass it.'

Of course I had to do so, but every time she asked me

a question after that, I made sure that I made a meal of the answer and went on and on intentionally.

On another day, a toddler came in with a tracheostomy and gastroenteritis and had to be 'specialled'. As I had nursed many children with a trachy I was put in with the child and I felt happy looking after her. Sister Richards would come into the cubicle and fuss around, saying this and that was not right, which made me bristle. It was unusual to have a child with a trachy on the ward and I sensed she was not confident dealing with one. On one particular day, we had to change the child's trachy tube to prevent mucus build-up and also for the sake of cleanliness. I had done this before and knew what to do, but Sister Richards came into the cubicle to help me. I gathered my equipment together and the spare tube and ensured that the trachy dilators were near at hand. These are used to keep the hole in the trachea open if the new tube does not immediately slip into place.

'Please can you hold her,' I asked Sister. She paused just a second too long. I knew then, instinctively, that she had not changed a trachy before.

My confidence was boosted and I proceeded to change the tube, tie the tapes to keep it in place and check that it was not too tight by putting two fingers inside the tape round the neck. The procedure made the child cough, but I knew that if I was swift, I would minimise any discomfort. I managed a particularly quick change and put a dressing under the tube to absorb any leakage of sputum. I then sat the child up and started to play with her doll to distract her. Sister Richards was silent throughout and I hoped she was suitably impressed.

'Well done,' she muttered.

Thankfully our relationship became more cordial after that. She let me get on with things without questioning my every move, which was a welcome relief.

When I first came to the observation ward, another thing hit me. The babies and children were all on diets that included puréed carrot which, I was told, 'binded the stools'. They were weighed every day and occasionally a nurse would misread the scales and chart the wrong weight; this was immediately picked up and questions were asked. I learnt a lot about dehydration, fluid loss and metabolic imbalance, as some of the children were critically ill when they first came into hospital. After fluid replacement via intravenous therapy, they soon perked up. Stools were often sent to the laboratory for culture and tested for sensitivity to antibiotics. As a result, I got to know the laboratory staff and found the lab a very mystical and intriguing place. The consultant there was doing specialist research into gastroenteritis, but we never heard the results. Despite my new wisdom, the attitude of Sister Richards left an impression on me. She was very distant and very rigid in her teaching and I vowed that if I progressed through the ranks I would try to be more approachable and understanding.

I enjoyed living in the nurses' home attached to GOSH, but I did miss my friends from Cambridge, like Cuth, who I caught up with when I was back home, which was only about three times a year. The weeks seemed to flash past, as life seemed so hectic with our respective careers. Even now I am retired, we still don't see each other as often as I had hoped because we are still so busy.

I found I made new nurse friends at the hostel quite easily and we would often talk about our experiences in a way that we couldn't with friends outside nursing or our families, not only because of confidentiality issues, but mostly because they didn't have the same understanding of our day-to-day lives and the unique pressure we were under.

I was relieved to be back at GOSH and one of the wards I really enjoyed was 2AB, the metabolic and endocrine ward. Some children had complex problems with their digestive systems and others had 'inborn errors of metabolism': an inability of the body to use certain nutrients in foods such as protein, because it lacks a specific enzyme. This is where such children would come to be treated. Children from all over the country with puzzling symptoms are sent to GOSH, so rare conditions seem to concentrate there. It means that the hospital doctors become skilled at detecting problems that might be regarded as undetectable elsewhere.

The wards were labelled by their floor at the time: one side was called AB and the other CD, so this ward stretched across one side of the building. By now – I was eight months in – I was getting used to complicated diagnoses, but when I arrived on the first day, I realised that they had a language of their own. I had yet more learning to do. If a baby was given the wrong feed, such as SMA baby feed or cow's milk, their blood chemistry would develop an imbalance and they would become unwell. How did the parents manage when their children went to nursery, birthday parties or, later, to school? The ward had a particular smell about it, like rotting food. I learnt that this was the 'chix' or 'chicken feed': an amino acid mixture, a controlled mixture of essential proteins to ensure a child's growth. The babies oozed it from their pores and, of course, it was present in their bowels and vomit.

One thing I was taught to watch out for on 2AB was Munchausen's syndrome. This is a form of child abuse in which a parent induces real or apparent symptoms of a disease in a child. It often manifested itself in stomach problems. In those days, rare metabolic syndromes were difficult to diagnose, but we were told to always be aware of them. Nowadays, we know much more about abnormal metabolic pathways, which can run in families, and some can be treated by avoiding certain foods. In Munchausen's cases generally, the child's symptoms do not fit a classic picture of a disease. It was therefore emphasised to us as students that we must always write everything down, including when the parents visited, or if any untoward events involving staff or parents occured. I was horrified when I first learnt about Munchausen's. How could someone deliberately hurt his or her child to get attention? Although it was rare, I knew it was possible for symptoms to go away once the child was in hospital. Where there was suspicion of the syndrome, the child would be 'specialled' throughout their stay.

Although I didn't nurse a child undergoing investigation for Munchausen's during this time, I became involved in cases later in my career and was grateful for this early awareness. The ward sister, Shirley Hensman, was a rather distant figure, who always seemed to be in a world of her own. She was very well informed about Munchausen's and also about metabolic pathways and congenital abnormal syndromes. I absorbed a lot from her about these illnesses.

There were many interesting consultants attached to this ward, but the one who stands out was Professor

Otto Wolff. He was a tall, slim and gentle-mannered man. He always took time to explain things and was genuinely interested in people. I became friendly with him later on in life and he had a charming wife. Long after he retired, he always attended the medical academic sessions at GOSH, and would take part in the debates promoting family-centred care. Professor Wolff always brought egotistical junior medical staff back down to earth with his wisdom.

One of the babies I remember vividly at that time was little Mario, a beautiful baby who had huge coffee-coloured eyes and eyelashes any girl would be proud of. He was admitted when he was only a few months old and had one of the rarer metabolic disorders, which meant he had to be fed every four hours, even during the night. It was essential that he had the right nutrients or else he would fit. As he was a slow feeder, each meal took around an hour-and-a-half, so it was frustrating when, towards the end, he pulled a face and vomited all over the floor and his cot. We would need to clean him up and start all over again. We had lots of other children who needed feeding regularly, so it was a good job that we worked as a team, otherwise we would never have finished.

When he was going through a good phase, Mario was a lovely child whose eyes sparkled when he smiled. As he got older, he would reach out of his cot with his little chubby hands whenever I was walking past. I was learning that some children affected you more than others, I don't know why. Perhaps it was simple chemistry. I really loved Mario, despite the difficulties of keeping him fed, and I felt challenged by him because I had to be patient and relaxed when caring for him.

I remember one evening, when I was tired and eager to get away because one of the other nurses had invited me to a party at her flat. It seemed that wherever there were nurses, there were plenty of invitations. I was due off duty at 9 p.m. and needed to go home and change, and put on some make-up to hide the huge black bags under my eyes. We were one nurse down on the ward and in order to make it to the party before 11 p.m., by which time everyone would probably be slightly the worse for wear, everything would need to run like clockwork. As I went to Mario's cot with his special feed, I was tempted to try to feed him quickly but stopped myself – I had made that mistake before. I told myself to be calm, relaxed and smiley, as if I had all the time in the world. So I meandered over, picked him up and played with him, making him giggle by tickling his tummy, before I even started spooning the feed into his little pink mouth. That evening my calmness paid off, and I made it to the party and had a great time. But often he would vomit, even if I fed him painfully slowly.

Mario stayed with us for about a year, an awfully long time in the world of a child. He was from a large Italian family and while his parents were fond of him, they only visited at weekends because they lived in Manchester and had six older children, all girls. His father, Stefano, a window cleaner, had his own business and so often had to work seven days a week. His mother, Isabella, felt she must be at home to cook, clean and care for her other children, and she also worked part-time in a nursery. Money was tight and the family could just about manage financially, but visiting the hospital was expensive. Even though they had been referred to the social worker for financial help with fares, it was still a stretch for all eight of them to take the train down to London.

It was perhaps even harder for Mario. We tried to let Stefano and Isabella take responsibility for the 'parenting' or caring side of things when they visited, as we always did with parents, but as time went on, the baby was obviously more used to being cared for by us.

One day, when Isabella visited with some of her children, Mario wouldn't stop crying. His siblings were shrieking and bickering and running round the ward, while Isabella shouted at them in Italian to stop making such a noise. She looked stressed and no matter what she did, Mario continued to wail. After half an hour of being jiggled up and down, he was crying so hard that he was violently sick all over himself and Isabella. He immediately quietened when I rushed over to help, and while we tried to make light of it and set about mopping them both up, it was obvious that Isabella knew that Mario would prefer to be with us. She looked all too relieved when visiting time was over and she could bundle up her children and make for home.

During these visits, Stefano and Isabella often spoke of their fears about how they would manage when their son eventually came home. I'm sure Mario sometimes picked up on those vibes, as he would stretch away from them, looking around for someone else to cuddle him. We tried to ignore it but it was hard for everybody.

When he was around eighteen months old, Mario's condition was stable; he was putting on weight and developing well. His care was discussed with his local hospital in Manchester and it was decided that he would be transferred there within the next month to make it easier for Stefano and Isabella and his siblings to visit him. The dietician had talked over with the new hospital the complicated diet Mario required, so they could stock up on the ingredients he needed, and the sister on the ward rang the local sister to discuss everything in detail.

For Stefano and Isabella, and a lot of other parents, GOSH had been the last resort in what must have been a very stressful time seeking a diagnosis. The removal of their child to their local hospital made them horribly apprehensive. But we had to make a break, otherwise Mario might be with us for years and other children would need his bed.

When the time came for him to leave, we dressed him in his best shirt and trousers, packed up all his toys and put everything in two large brown suitcases. Stefano and Isabella had arrived the day before and spent the night in the parents' accommodation. They knew that any variation in Mario's strict diet could spell disaster and bombarded us with questions: Would the local hospital know what to do? Would the doctors know how to handle him? What if he started having fits again?

We tried to reassure them, telling them the local doctors could always ring us and that they, too, could pick up the phone if they were worried.

I found the situation difficult too. While I was happy that Mario was making progress and moving closer to his family, I was apprehensive about exactly the same things that his parents were: Would his new carers be diligent enough? Would they understand him in the way that I did? I didn't know.

We rarely found out what happened to the children when they left our care, however long they had been with us, which was difficult to come to terms with. Sometimes parents kept in touch, but more often than not they didn't. Perhaps we were a reminder of what must have been a very traumatic time for them. Stefano and Isabella never did write or call and I hoped this was a good sign. I often think about that smiley, sicky baby. I hope he thrived.

# 6

## Laughter and Fear

After my time in the nurses' home, I was keen to move into a flat, and finally found what I was looking for near Lancaster Gate, not far from Marble Arch. The area was as smart then as it is now and it cost quite a large chunk of my wages, but I loved it. I shared the flat with Jenny, Joan and Mary, who were in my set at GOSH, and Moira, who was Mary's childhood friend and was nursing at the Middlesex Hospital. Three of us shared one of the bedrooms and the other two slept in the second one. The nearest station was Holborn and it took about twenty minutes to get to the hospital on the Central Line. I enjoyed hopping on the tube after work and feeling that I was getting away from it all; something I had never really managed when I was living next door to GOSH. We all enjoyed living in the Marble Arch area and felt we could entertain our friends properly in the new flat. I forged a particularly strong bond with Joan, a petite dark-haired girl who had a wicked sense of humour. On nights when we didn't fancy cooking, we would eat at cheap restaurants in Bayswater or on the Edgware Road, and then go to a club where we would dance until we were exhausted. We all found that this was a good way of releasing the tensions of work. Like my previous flatshares, there was a real sense of camaraderie between us. We all understood each other well and looked out for one another. I never had a boyfriend during this time, as there was never anyone I liked enough, but I was so caught up in my work that I didn't mind.

Practical jokes were a key part of my life at GOSH. We were always trying to catch each other out and better the last prank. One night on the ward, I was bored and everything was ticking over nicely, so I called my flat-mate, Joan, who was in the private ward. She had been moaning earlier in the night that everything was quiet where she was, too.

'Nurse, it's Sister here,' I said, trying to change my voice so that she wouldn't recognise me. 'We have a baby with a diaphragmatic hernia coming in. Please make the necessary preparations.'

'Yes, Sister, I will,' she said, sounding alarmed, and hung up. Oh, how funny, I thought; she wasn't going to be twiddling her thumbs now. No more leisurely cups of tea and biscuits for her.

I forgot about Joan for a while as I got on with my various duties. Regardless of how quiet things were on the ward, there were always things to be done.

After about an hour, the phone rang and I suddenly remembered my clever little joke. As I had heard nothing more from Joan, I called her again.

'Nurse, it's Sister, how are the preparations coming along?'

'I have called the anaesthetist and let the theatre know. The surgeon has been notified. They are all on their way in now,' she said.

Suddenly I felt embarrassed and realised that perhaps this wasn't very funny after all. I don't know why, but I hadn't expected Joan to involve other people, I just imagined her rushing around like a headless chicken. I hadn't thought it through at all.

'Joan. It's me, Susan. It was a joke. I know you said you were quiet so I thought ...'

'Well that's not funny! I've woken up the doctor, the surgeon, everyone. I've got to go and undo this mess.'

She hung up abruptly and I was left wondering what I had done. I felt terrible and really hoped it wouldn't ruin my career progression.

Sure enough, the night sister was soon on the warpath. I knew I had to come clean, so I owned up and apologised profusely. I felt awful.

'Well, you'll need to say sorry to the surgeon and doctor in the morning. They were woken up,' she said.

'I will,' I said, my face flaming. 'I just didn't think. It was a really stupid thing to do. I'm so sorry.'

After getting everything ready on the ward for the day staff, I sheepishly presented myself the following day and apologised to both the men involved. They were surprisingly good-natured about it considering they had been woken unnecessarily and I had certainly learnt my lesson.

A few days after I obtained my registration for sick children's nursing, I saw the post of night sister advertised. In order to get ahead in my career I knew I needed to do a good stint on night duty, and perhaps for as long as a year. It would be continuous, but at least I would get a few days off in a row and could have some social life. My body clock would just have to cope, although it usually took me twenty-four to forty-eight hours to adjust. At least I would not be compelled to finish the year if another job came up. Everyone would understand.

After an interview, I was offered the post and within a week reported to the night sister's office. After being cocooned by the relative safety of the ward, I now had to start thinking about the hospital as a whole: Were all the wards staffed with enough nurses? Who and where were the sick children? Would every nurse get a tea and dinner break? Were there enough staff to give the intravenous drugs? Who would cover the admissions unit? I was now responsible for all these things.

I was given a bleep and people could contact me via the switchboard. The telephone number came up on the bleep so I could be contacted while on duty. At first this seemed strange. When it went off, a volley of thoughts rushed through my head: Who would be on the end of the telephone? What would the call be about? Would I know what to do? My colleagues were very supportive and helped me to adjust to the new role.

One night, during my first fortnight in charge, I received an urgent summons to the admissions unit from one of the sisters. Although we didn't have an accident and emergency unit at GOSH, some anxious parents brought their sick children in overnight, hoping to be seen by a doctor. Before transferring them to the nearest casualty department, at University College Hospital, we had to examine them and take a history and their observations – temperature, pulse and respirations – to assess whether they needed urgent treatment, or could wait to see their GP the following day. Sometimes, those needing immediate treatment would be admitted to the ward. We would see babies with heart disease, renal abnormalities, gastroenteritis, or infectious diseases such as chickenpox. While most children got over chickenpox easily, others might develop neurological abnormalities such as encephalitis, which is swelling on the brain, or complications such as a chest infection, which could be life-threatening.

On this occasion, the new arrival wasn't a child with its parents, but a heavily pregnant woman who seemed to be in labour. As it wasn't that long since I had done my midwifery course in Bristol, I felt equipped to deal with the problem. I rushed down to the admissions room where a small woman in a pink anorak with the hood up was groaning and clutching her enlarged belly. She had her back towards me.

'Ugggggghhhhhh,' she moaned. 'They've started. The contractions are so painful. Please help me.'

'How many weeks pregnant are you?' I asked. I looked her in the eye as she winced in agony.

'I'm thirty-eight weeks. I was just round the corner, going home after having dinner out with my friends, when the contractions started. Ugggghhhhhhhhhh. I need some pain relief. I can't do this.'

I continued with my questioning: Was it her first baby? Where was she booked in to have her baby? Had she had any problems during her pregnancy? How frequent were her contractions?

'Ugggggghhhhhhhhhh,' she screamed, hanging on to a nearby chair for support. At the rate she was contracting it looked as if I might be delivering her baby right there and then, in the admissions room.

'God, this is awful. Helppppppp.'

'Have your waters broken?' I continued, running through a mental checklist of things I needed to know, while thinking about where we could put her if she really was going to have her baby here.

Then her moaning stopped abruptly. She turned to look at me and burst into a loud, raucous laugh.

'What?' I looked at her again. There was definitely something familiar about those green eyes.

'Susan! It's me.'

*I* had been had this time.

It was Joan. She pulled a large cushion from under her anorak and was bent over in stitches.

I started giggling too. I couldn't believe it; I had been looking at her face the entire time, but had been so focused on the job in hand that I hadn't recognised her. She had done a brilliant job and I quipped that she should consider a change of career, from nursing to acting. I felt a bit of a fool but entered into the joke – and started plotting my revenge.

Night duty was so busy that we often worked through our breaks. However, at about 4 a.m., the sisters would meet to catch up, have a cup of tea and report to the person in charge. Then the daily routine would start all over again at around 5 a.m., with drugs rounds, helping nurses who were busy and checking on the very sick children. We would go full pelt until it was time to go off duty, which was normally around 8.30 a.m. It might be later if we were looking after a child who required immediate attention. If the day nurse in charge of a ward was late, or went off sick, we were left to cope until a senior nurse could be found.

We often saw a lot of the same illnesses, especially during the autumn and winter months, such as respiratory syncytial virus (RSV). This infection causes bronchiolitis, which could be very serious for young babies. I remember a three-month-old, Katy, being brought in with respiratory distress. It was November and the weather was bitterly cold outside; everyone was coughing into their hankies and moaning. Katy's mother,

Heather, a much older mum in her mid-forties, had seen a doctor in the renal clinic at outpatients the previous day, because the baby was being investigated for renal abnormalities and had shown signs of a chest infection. She was told to bring her daughter back if she got any worse.

At about 2 a.m. Heather rushed in dressed in a Barbour jacket and pyjama bottoms, carrying Katy. Although she looked a timid sort of lady, who didn't meet your eye when she spoke to you, Heather was shouting as she entered the admissions unit. Two bleary-eyed children, a boy and a girl of about nine and ten, were with her. The girl was crying and hanging on to her teddy and the boy looked half asleep.

'She's wheezing and looked all floppy,' Heather exclaimed, cradling her baby. 'I was up late and went into her room to check on her. She looked as white as a ghost.'

Katy was assessed and admitted to a cubicle on Cohen, the infectious diseases ward. The child required a 'special'; she was put in an oxygen tent with the head of the cot raised and quarter-hourly observations for her temperature, pulse and respirations were taken.

'Is she going to be alright?' Heather asked, tears running down her cheeks. 'I mean, I know she had the kidney problems but what is this about? Is my baby alright?'

I tried to calm her down and offered her a cup of tea, but she wasn't interested.

'My husband Brian is on his way,' she said. 'He was away on a conference up north somewhere but I've told him to get his sorry arse down here right now.' It was a shock to hear those words coming from the mouth of a woman who looked as if she couldn't say boo to a goose.

'Do you want a sit-down in the waiting room?'

'No, I'm staying here. I've waited eight years to have another baby. I'm not letting her out of my sight.'

'I'll take the children in there,' I said. 'I can spare someone and they can sit with her.'

We put up two Z-Beds in the waiting room so that the children could rest. I learnt that these two kids were from Heather's previous marriage and Katy was a much-wanted third child with her new husband.

As the 'special' continued to take the baby's observations, Katy was making awful grunting noises like an animal in pain and her nostrils were flaring, all the signs of acute distress. The doctor had put up a drip and told us he was available if we needed him. I checked that the resuscitation trolley was nearby and there was a re-breathing bag with an airway by the bed – it was clear that this little girl wasn't at all well. Her face was still pale and her ribs were sucking inwards as she breathed. She was also bubbling at the mouth and required suction. Because I was worried, I approached the doctor who was at the end of the ward.

'Doctor, I think she should be admitted to intensive care,' I said. 'She's got intercostal recession and is bubbling at the mouth. I'm concerned she is going to get worse.'

Just as the doctor opened his mouth to reply, the emergency bell rang out and we ran to the cubicle.

'What's happening?' Heather shouted. One of the nurses led her out of the cubicle as it started filling up with people.

The nurse had put the re-breathing bag over Katy's mouth and was squeezing the bag to inflate her lungs.

'She stopped breathing and was going blue,' she said.

'Right, put out an emergency 5555 call,' I instructed. This was the code at GOSH which connected to the telephonist who would alert the emergency team.

I took Katy's pulse – it was a little slow, but was rising and colour was returning to her face as the nurse pumped oxygen into her.

'I'm going to intubate,' the doctor said. This meant putting a tube into the trachea, so I got the equipment ready. The tube slipped gently into Katy's windpipe and the re-breathing bag was attached.

When the emergency team arrived, including the resident assistant physician (RAP), an anaesthetist and the senior night sister, we explained what had happened and it was decided to put the baby on a ventilator. As she seemed more settled, the anaesthetist went to fetch this and I went to see Heather who had been waiting anxiously in the waiting room with the children.

'Thank God it's you. Is she okay? What's happening?'

'She's stable. We're helping her to breathe with a ventilator. The doctor will be in as soon as he can to talk to you.'

She looked me straight in the eye. 'Is she going to die? Tell me straight.'

I was as honest as possible; I knew that was the right way to respond. It always is.

'It's probably RSV, respiratory syncytial virus. Babies can be very ill with it and recover completely, but the next twenty-four to forty-eight hours will be hard,' I told her.

The doctor then came in to give Heather some more details and explained that the ventilator would breathe air in and out of her child's lungs until her condition stabilised.

'I'll come back and take you to Katy once she is settled,' I told her.

I went back to the ward, where the doctors were sorting out the ventilator and adjusting the dials. Katy was a better colour and seemed stable now she had been sedated and the machine was breathing for her. I checked that the nurse was happy and knew what she was doing, then I explained to Heather what the tube and ventilator looked like, before taking her to the cubicle: seeing one for the first time can sometimes be quite a shock. She was tearful and shaking.

As we entered the cubicle, she burst into tears. 'She's just so small,' she wept. I put my arm around her.

'Can you see how much more settled she is?' I said. 'Her colour is much better.'

'Yes, but the ventilator – it's so big and scary-looking.'

Heather sat with Katy for a few minutes, stroking her tiny fingers and sobbing, until I took her back to the waiting room, where I made her a strong cup of tea. It was about 5 a.m. by then and I knew that once the world woke up, she might begin to feel a tiny bit better; everything is always amplified at night.

'You can go back to the cubicle whenever you like. There will be a nurse with Katy all the time,' I told her.

Heather's two children were asleep next to us, but started to stir as we spoke in quiet voices.

'Mummy, is baby Katy okay?' I heard one of them ask in a small voice.

'Pray for your little sister as she is very ill. She may die,' Heather said.

I thought this was a bit blunt, but I wanted to do the right thing and suggested that maybe later I could show them all the hospital chapel. I knew Heather was

Catholic from the information she had given me on admission.

'Yes, children. You must pray for your sister. For her to be well again,' she said.

Later, I took Heather back to see Katy and she didn't want to leave her. I felt I had to follow through the idea of praying with the two children so, after checking that all was well, I took them to the chapel just along the corridor from the ward.

It was built in 1875, two years after the hospital originally opened, and is visually stunning. Although small, it is elaborately decorated in Byzantine style, with stained-glass windows depicting the Nativity, the childhood of Christ and biblical scenes. Soft toys are always dotted around the window sills and candles burn brightly near an altar low enough for children to kneel at. For all these years, it has been a place to which people can go with their emotions, their fear, hope, despair or sorrow, and find some kind of solace.

I held the children's hands as we entered through the wooden doors and they made the sign of the cross on their small chests. I was not very religious in my youth; in fact, I only started going to church when I converted to Catholicism before I married my husband, John, in my fifties.

The pews in the chapel, which are stained black, are small enough for children to sit on, and we went to one in the front and knelt down. I then said a little prayer for Katy, for them and their mother and stepfather, and they chorused 'Amen' at the end.

'Now, shall we say the Lord's Prayer?' I asked and we recited it all together.

'Nurse, I'm scared,' the little girl whimpered. 'Do you think God will help?'

'I'm sure he will,' I replied. 'Why don't you write him a message in the chapel memorial book?'

This book holds hundreds of messages from patients, siblings and parents, and sits near the entrance to the chapel. I collected it, along with a pen, and gave it first to the girl.

'Just write whatever you want,' I said. 'God will read it.'

She took the book from me, her hands trembling.

'Please God, make my sister better and stop my mummy crying,' she wrote slowly, in spidery letters.

The boy then took it and added: 'Please God, don't let my sister die. I love you.'

'Well done,' I said, suddenly filled with emotion. I really felt for them both.

'Do you want to go back to your mum now?' They both nodded pensively.

I held their small hands again as we walked back to the ward and left them in the playroom, while I went to tell Heather that we had been to the chapel. She seemed pleased.

'How is Katy?' I asked.

'She seems more stable.'

'Perhaps they could come and see their sister?' I suggested.

When they came into the cubicle, the girl climbed on to her mother's lap, sucking her thumb. The boy sat on a spare chair by the bed.

'Why are there so many tubes?' the little girl asked.

'That's to help Katy breathe,' I said. 'She just needs a bit of help at the moment because she isn't very well.'

The girl popped her thumb back in and seemed satisfied that all was well.

A couple of hours later Heather's husband, Brian, who looked younger than her, arrived, flustered and panicked. She seemed to be angry with him and, rather than turning to her husband for support, took her anger out on him – something that I saw on many occasions during my time at GOSH.

'You should've come back after the conference,' Heather shouted. 'Katy is so small still. I was on my own. How could you? Fun, was it? I hope it was worth it.'

'Heather...' Brian went to embrace his wife, but Heather turned away from him.

I think a lot of mothers felt that their husbands couldn't possibly understand the pain they were going through.

I told Brian exactly what was happening to Katy and he seemed to accept my explanation. Then I took them both back to the cubicle. The nurse knew that if anything changed, they could find me by bleeping me.

Before I went off duty I went to see the family again. They had managed to get a little sleep and I told them they were welcome to have breakfast in the hospital canteen, and how to find it. The doctor would be seeing them during his morning rounds.

When I came on duty the next night, I was pleased to hear that Katy was still stable. I went to the ward and found only Heather there, looking tired. She explained that Brian had taken the children home with him so they could get some proper rest.

'How is Katy?' I asked.

'A little better,' Heather said, a faraway look in her eyes. 'You know, I fought so long to have her. I don't think I could cope if anything bad happened to her.'

'What have the doctors told you?'

'She'll be on a ventilator for a few days and then they'll try to take her off.'

'Babies are remarkably resilient, you know. I'm off duty for a few days after tonight so I may not see you again.' I knew I wouldn't be back in the hospital for four days – a critical time in Katy's care.

'Thank you.' She hugged me and I squeezed her back. 'For everything you've done for us and for looking after the children and taking them to the chapel. I think perhaps God was listening.'

Many religious people found much comfort in the chapel and their faith while at GOSH – Heather was clearly one of them.

I felt sure Katy would be okay and I felt tempted to say, 'She'll be fine.' However, I had learnt that this wasn't necessarily the right thing to do. A respiratory arrest can cause brain damage if the brain is deprived of oxygen for too long. I felt sure we had caught Katy in time and had my fingers crossed.

I thought about Katy many times as I pottered around London during my days off, meeting up with friends, catching up on my laundry and trying to relax. When I went on duty four nights later, Katy wasn't mentioned in the ward report. I didn't know whether this was a good or bad sign.

Afterwards, I went straight to the ward and asked about her. The nurse told me that she had been extubated. In other words, she had been taken off the ventilator and the breathing tube had been taken out. She was feeding well and expected to go home the following day.

I looked in on Katy and she was rosy-faced and gurgling. Heather wasn't there; the nurse said she was much happier and had gone home to get some sleep, but that Katy's siblings had visited her several times. I knew I wouldn't see the family again. I felt so relieved. Children are up and down so quickly, but at least this one had recovered and her poor mother's anxiety had been dispelled. It could so easily have not been the case.

# 7

# Days at the Whittington

My night sister duty passed quickly and I started looking for a day sister's post, but there were none at GOSH at the time. The Whittington Hospital in north London was advertising for a sister on one of its paediatric units, so I applied. I was interviewed by a new paediatrician called Max Friedman, who seemed very forward-thinking. I enjoyed his enthusiasm and found his questions interesting. However, the nursing officer in charge seemed a bit staid and asked unnecessary questions: Why did I want to come to the Whittington? What was my experience with children? This information was all to be found on my application form. There were no questions about play therapy, resident parents or new nursing practices.

I started at the Whittington in 1970, when I was twenty-five years old. The medical paediatric unit was in the Archway wing. There were two Nightingale wards in the hospital and one baby ward. Each ward had eighteen beds and two cubicles. It was busy and noisy and seemed chaotic all the time. Many admissions occurred daily, such as children with meningitis, chest infections, overdoses, diabetes, urinary tract infections, gastroenteritis, and sometimes those who had been neglected by their parents or even deliberately harmed.

I soon got to know the other ward sisters who were very supportive, but I was disturbed by the poor nursing care I witnessed at times. Everyone appeared to accept things the way they were.

One ritual that shocked me was the medicine round. During my first day, one of the nurses on duty asked me to check the drugs before they were administered. The medicines were neatly laid out in 5ml-glass measures on top of the prescription charts, the solutions all different colours, but there was no bottle giving the name of the medicine or the dosage. On looking more closely, I was not even sure that the dosages were correct.

When I pointed out that this was not the right way to check medicines, the nurse replied, 'But we always do it this way.'

Not while I'm Sister you don't, I thought.

I made her throw away the medicines, wash the glasses and start all over again. I was not popular and I was aware that some of the more junior nurses were talking about me behind my back. It took a long time to stop the practice, as I knew they would revert to a quicker but certainly more dangerous tradition in my absence.

Another time, when I came on duty at 7.30 a.m., I could see that the ward had been busy. Before handover, I went to see a fifteen-month-old child who was lying in a cot within an oxygen tent. I lifted the side of the tent to examine him and thought he looked very drowsy, with laboured breathing. His colour was pink, but his pulse and blood pressure were higher than normal.

'How has he been?' I asked the night nurse.

'He's been really sleepy, he seems very tired. I'm sorry the drip isn't going as fast as it should, but I've tried to make it go quicker. It's on 125ml per hour.'

I was shocked. How fast? I wondered. Thank God it wasn't going at that rate as it was far too fast.

When I checked the child, I suspected he was suffering from fluid overload and might be in heart failure or have cerebral oedema, where water collects on the brain.

I asked a colleague to call a doctor immediately and was told that the doctor on duty that morning was the senior house officer.

A young, tired-looking fellow soon arrived to look at the baby.

'I think he needs a tube into his windpipe to help him to breathe,' he said.

That wasn't right, I thought. The baby needed a diuretic to get rid of the water.

'I disagree,' I said. I was confident I was right.

'Let's see what the registrar says,' the doctor conceded.

The registrar took thirty minutes to arrive because he lived some distance from the hospital. We explained the situation to him and after assessing the child he turned to me.

'You're right,' he said. We gave him a diuretic and over the next few hours the boy's condition improved. I was thankful that I had spoken out.

During one ward round, the consultant enquired if the children who had meningitis, or were unconscious, were being turned regularly. I felt very hurt by his question.

'Yes, of course,' I said haughtily and we moved on. It was such a fundamental practice that it was second nature to me. No one who knew what they were doing would allow a pressure sore to occur through not turning a child who was unable to move. I would have been mortified if this had occurred. But over time I realised that if something was not written down in the patients' records, then it probably didn't get done. I understood now why I had been asked about turning and later apologised to the consultant. I told him he need never ask me about this again. Under my watch, turning would be a regular procedure.

After the Salmon Report was published in 1966, the world of nursing started to change. This report recommended a change in the senior nursing structure within hospitals and effectively brought an end to the traditional matron's role. Instead, the report proposed that each hospital had a chief nursing officer, reporting to the hospital management, and a hierarchy of principal nursing officers, senior nursing officers, nursing officers, then ward sisters. The aim was to raise the profile of the profession in hospital management and ensure that senior nurses had access to management training. Some of the disciplinarian structures were being relaxed, with straight shifts rather than split shifts being introduced, and part-time working. Another former taboo – married nursing sisters – was also now tolerated.

The results of the report were starting to become apparent in all hospitals around this time and I know the nursing officers were unpopular with the nurses themselves.

The nursing officer in overall charge of the paediatric wards at the Whittington was a Miss Andrews and I found her both aloof and critical. She was constantly asking me questions and casting doubt on my decisions: Why had I allocated this particular nurse to these patients? What was that nurse doing with the potty? Why were the toys out so much and making such a mess?

I didn't want to fall out with my boss and tried to be pleasant and understanding of her criticism; I was still young and felt that maybe I had more to learn. However, when there was only one other nurse on a busy ward at times, I felt she was being unreasonable. I failed to gain her support in my campaign for more resources. When I complained about standards, she said she found me argumentative and made no effort to help me manage the other nurses.

I always encouraged parents and siblings to visit and had turned a side room into a parents' room where they could make themselves tea or coffee. I knew it was important that they were involved with their children's care, but Miss Andrews said she felt that visitors were in the way.

'They crowd the ward and bring in infection. Please ask them to leave,' she would tell me.

She was also of the school of thought that play was a waste of time when children were ill. At that time, it was a relatively new innovation in paediatric wards. Eve was the play leader and she and I became friendly as we shared the same values. On some of our days off, we attended Anna Freud's child development classes in Hampstead. One of the pioneers of child psychotherapy, Anna Freud proposed that play expressed a child's unconscious desires, thoughts and emotions. This was the first time I had ventured outside the hospital setting to seek further education and I found it really helpful, as well as giving me a different perspective. I felt that play could be a good educational tool for both parents and children. Being in hospital was a frightening experience for many – children are uprooted from their homes, parents and families, and are thrust into an alien environment where they are prodded, made to swallow strange-tasting substances and attached to weird machines. Eve was good at introducing equipment such as stethoscopes and syringes for injections into the children's play, to show them what was going to happen to them. How to give teddy an anaesthetic was a favourite game: one minute he would be jumping about, and the next moment he would be lying down for a nice 'sleep'!

Drawing and painting, although a little messy, was also a medium for children to express their feelings. Some paintings were dark and distressing, indicating that the child was suffering, even though showing no outward signs of it. A child psychologist also attended ward meetings at which these things could be discussed. Eve attended too and would participate in offering the care which some of the children lacked.

We had one real success on the ward with Helen, a child of seven, who had newly diagnosed diabetes and required daily insulin injections. Helen was a very 'girlie' little girl, with long, fine blonde hair down to her waist.

'It's like Rapunzel's,' she would tell us and insist that we brushed it a hundred times every night before she went to sleep. This was a job in itself because she would complain if we tugged at the knots.

Helen hated needles of any kind and would let out an ear-piercing scream if any of us even mentioned them. She was also quite a madam and the other nurses and I found that we could not discuss anything with her. She made it quite clear that she didn't want to listen by turning her head and sticking her lightly freckled nose in the air and closing her eyes, as if we were all completely invisible.

'Not listening,' she would say. 'Not listening. I can't hear you.'

After a few days of trying to talk to her about her injections and getting the same response, I asked Eve if she could help me.

'Oh, I do love a challenge,' she said with a laugh, as I relayed what had happened so far.

I watched Eve as discreetly as I could while busying myself with other jobs. She began by getting to know Helen and letting her help play with some of the younger children on the ward; their discussion of princesses and fairy tales was a real hit.

Eve then explained how she played doctors and nurses with the other children and showed Helen the instruments in the smart doctor's bag, such as a stethoscope, thermometer and reflex hammer. She also showed Helen a syringe, but it didn't have a needle; these were not allowed in play for obvious reasons.

Eve then went to fetch an orange. She carefully showed Helen how to give an injection with a real needle and then let her do one herself, into the orange. The little girl laughed as she pressed the plunger into the orange's stiff flesh; she thought it was really funny.

This went on for a few days, to gain Helen's confidence, and each time she squeezed the hard plastic plunger, she looked very pleased with herself. Helen was also shown special books about children with diabetes, who needed to be aware of what they ate and follow their parents' instructions about how to manage their illness.

Midway through the first week, Eve asked Helen to draw a number of pictures.

'Where is your pancreas where insulin is made? Draw it for me,' or 'Can you describe in a picture how an injection feels?' she would say, handing over some crayons and paper.

Helen was quite a good artist and everyone dutifully admired her pictures, which we pinned up by her bed. Already Helen was beginning to accept things more readily and was less anxious. She had been having the insulin injections every day, but was still reluctant to do them herself.

'Give her time,' Eve said.

After about a week of practising on the orange, I went over to where Eve was sitting with Helen and asked her if she was ready to do an injection on herself.

'Yes,' she said quietly. I could tell she was still very reluctant.

'Great. Shall we try now?'

I passed her the equipment and she drew the correct amount of insulin up into the syringe. Then she sat on the chair next to her bed and lifted up her skirt to expose her bare thigh.

Suddenly she froze and tears welled in her eyes.

'I don't want to . . .' she whimpered.

'Take your time,' Eve told her gently. 'Pretend it's that orange. Here's the alcohol swab to clean your leg.'

Helen took it and wiped it over her pale skin.

'Here is the syringe to give the injection,' Eve continued, quietly and calmly.

Helen took it, breathed in and put the needle into her flesh with wide eyes.

'Now push the plunger in,' said Eve and Helen followed her words, all the time looking really worried.

'Take the needle out,' Eve said.

Helen did so and exhaled loudly. She had been holding

her breath. Eve then put the cotton wool ball over the injection site and gently rubbed it.

'It's all over. Well done!' Eve said, cuddling her.

'Well done, Helen. Hurrah!' I added.

Next day, we went through the process again. Helen appeared calmer and more confident, and after that she never looked back. Shortly afterwards she was able to go home, where a district nurse would check that all was well with the injections. I did wonder how she would manage during her teenage years, when many diabetics become erratic in controlling their blood sugar, but I knew we were over this particular hump. Neither the district nurse nor Helen's mother rang to say it was not going well, so I presume Eve's magic had worked.

As time wore on, I still felt picked on and constantly undermined by Miss Andrews. The fact that I was unhappy at work affected my personal life and I often found myself questioning my decisions and abilities. I knew I was doing my best, but it never seemed to be enough for her. It is horrible not having support from your seniors and some days I felt overwrought and unhappy.

On one occasion, I was on duty alongside a very competent third-year student. I asked her if she would look after a little boy called Lenny who was on a ventilator. She was happy to do so, as she knew she could ask me for help if she needed it. I then set about giving care to the other children.

Soon afterwards Miss Andrews walked in. She looked up and down the ward and strode over to me.

'Why are you not looking after Lenny?' she asked, in her abrupt way.

I tried to remain calm.

'I think I can probably work quicker looking after the other children and asking the parents to do certain things while I supervise them. The nurse I've allocated to Lenny is very competent in what she is doing. She knows to ask if she has any queries.'

'I disagree, Sister Macqueen. You must look after him yourself,' she instructed.

I felt this was an accident waiting to happen. I was furious at being undermined like this, particularly as I was rushed off my feet. My neck and face flushed red and my heart started hammering. I knew I had to confront the problem head-on and before I had a chance to think about it, I called her over.

'Please can we have a chat in the office?' I asked, as we marched down the ward.

She closed the door behind us. Remain calm but firm, I told myself. This confrontation certainly wasn't planned, but I was at my wits' end.

'Please, Miss Andrews, I know what I am doing and I really would appreciate it if you stopped criticising everything I do. It would be far more useful if you rolled up your sleeves and helped me out instead.'

I had never argued with my manager before, but she did not seem to have an ounce of empathy for the children or their parents, and certainly not for the nurses. She remained silent – not that she could get a word in anyway!

'Right, I must get on now, if you will just let me do my job,' I said, before walking out and leaving her standing there, open-mouthed.

When the next shift arrived, I was pleased that all the major work was completed and all the drugs had been given out, which was sometimes not the case. I was dreading seeing Miss Andrews again and wondered if I should apologise to her. It was one of those moments that felt a bit surreal, as if maybe I had imagined the whole thing. I went over and over it in my head.

That night, when I got home, I couldn't be bothered to make myself any dinner. Instead I put together a limp sandwich and a cup of coffee and sat numbly in front of the television with Joan.

'Sue, are you okay? You look like you're on another planet,' she said.

'I've had a horrible day,' I replied and relayed the story of Miss Andrews.

'She sounds like one of the old school,' Joan said. 'And good for you for standing up to her. It sounds as if she needs taking down a peg or two.'

'I just don't know if I did the right thing. What if she makes my life even more difficult now?'

'I don't think she will. She's probably one of those women who is more mouth than action. Try not to worry,' Joan continued.

'I hope I came across as strong and determined rather than rude,' I added nervously.

That night I went to bed with the conversation going round and round in my head. I decided I needed to speak to Miss Andrews again about my aims and apologise if I had been impolite.

The following day, when she came on the ward, I finished what I was doing and went over to her.

'I'm sorry for yesterday. I don't want our relationship to suffer, but I still stick by the fact that things have to change,' I said. 'We need more staff on the ward and standards have to improve.'

'I'll see what I can do,' was her clipped response.

She remained aloof, but less critical, and our relationship remained professional – but only just.

Another incident at the Whittington occurred on the adjoining ward, where the sister told me she had a two-year-old girl with a fractured femur, the bone in her upper leg. The sister wanted to borrow a Gallows traction set, which was made up of adhesive plaster and rope. The child's legs were hung up by applying the plaster on both sides, and the rope was then tied to a wooden frame above the child's hips for several weeks, so that the body acted as counter-traction; the weight of the body extended the bone and acted as a traction so that it could heal without deformity. I gave Sister only one traction set, assuming she already had one she could use. A few hours later, when I went into her ward to speak to her, I noticed that the child had only one leg hanging up. I asked her if she needed another set because both legs should be applied in traction.

'Oh,' she said, 'I haven't done one before.' I then realised that there was more ignorance on the unit than I had thought.

The defining moment for me was in my second year at the Whittington. It was Christmastime and my ward was full because we had merged two wards together. I left on Christmas Eve having sorted out, wrapped and labelled all the children's presents, with Eve's help. We had put them in a large sack and instructed the night nurses to hand them out when the children woke up, saying that Santa and his reindeer had dropped them off.

To me, it was important that the parents and children had a reasonable time, if they were to be stuck in hospital over the Christmas period. The ward had been decorated on 23 December; we couldn't do it any earlier because everything got so dusty. At the end of the ward was a Christmas tree, with brightly coloured baubles hanging from it. Each bed frame was wrapped in tinsel, and paper-chains, which the children had helped to make, were strung across the ceilings and windows. The nurses also deserved to enjoy the occasion, so we made the office into a retreat where we could serve some festive food and offer alcoholic drinks to parents and any members of staff who were not working. A small radio in the corner played jolly Christmas songs.

When I arrived in the morning, full of Christmas spirit and looking forward to a good day, I was surprised to find that the ward looked exactly the same as it had on the previous evening: there were no presents or wrapping paper to be seen, the children were not yet up and dressed, and in the middle of the ward there was an ashtray full of cigarette butts. The night nurses hadn't even hidden the evidence of a night clearly spent having a good time and smoking rather, than doing what needed to be done on the ward.

I almost couldn't believe my eyes. The situation deeply shocked and saddened me. Not only that. Some of the children were nursed in oxygen tents and to light a cigarette anywhere near them could have caused an explosion. How could anyone put children at risk like that?

I felt a huge wall of rage build up inside me and was so upset I almost didn't know what to say.

I called the two nurses over. 'What's this ashtray?' I demanded. They were both silent; they knew it was wrong.

'Do you not realise you were putting the children, and yourselves, at risk by smoking on the ward?'

They shrugged their shoulders and looked at the floor, like naughty schoolchildren. It was as if they didn't care and just wanted to go home.

I was worried I might crack, so turned on my heel and got on with the day, trying to make up for their behaviour.

Later in the day, Max Friedman, the consultant, dressed up as Father Christmas with a snowy-white beard and a red suit. Most of the children loved it, their eyes were on stalks as he entered the ward with the famous 'Ho ho ho! Who's been good this year?' We jingled some bells in the distance and asked the children if they could hear the reindeer. Max then went round to each bed with the presents that should been given out earlier. Carols rang out from the radio and we all remained upbeat as we went about our work.

At lunchtime, the trolley with the Christmas food came up to the ward, containing turkey, roast potatoes and all the trimmings. Max then proceeded to carve the bird and we served lunch to those children who were able to eat and their parents. For hospital food, it wasn't at all bad. This was followed by a hearty serving of Christmas pudding, finished off with a glass, or four, of sherry for the parents. We tried to make it a proper Christmas for the children, even though they weren't at home with their families and friends, and hoped it helped to alleviate their parents' anxiety. Christmas is such a poignant time.

After we had cleared everything away and settled the children, giving them their drugs and any treatment, the nurses took it in turns to have their lunch, which had been saved for them. Some had brought from home extra delicacies like Turkish Delight and dried fruit, which they shared around. Everyone seemed to enjoy themselves, although for the trained staff, who stayed on duty the whole day, it was the equivalent of a double shift. I went home that night knowing I had done the best I could, but still saddened and unnerved by what I had seen in the morning.

For me, it was the final straw.

# 8

# A Ward of My Own

I went back to GOSH in 1972 at the age of twenty-seven. I felt apprehensive but excited to be back in a stimulating environment and there was still so much to learn. Elsewhere in the United Kingdom, it was a difficult time; there were economic and political problems aplenty, including a miners' strike, and the Troubles in Northern Ireland had reached a new peak. That year will perhaps be best remembered for the terrible events of Bloody Sunday in Londonderry.

My new job was as ward sister on Cohen Ward. I was very conscious that I was taking over from a long-term and highly respected resident who was retiring. I was also apprehensive because Cohen was a ward I hadn't worked on as a student, and so I felt under particular pressure to prove myself and do a good job. Above all, I saw it as a great opportunity and was excited about having a ward of my own.

I was also delighted to collect my new uniform. It was out with the pink one and in with a light blue, fine-dog-toothed dress with a high collar edged with white piping, and short sleeves. I wore brown stockings and shoes, plus a white apron and a white frilly hat, which I secured in place with matching white hairgrips.

Seeing myself in the mirror for the first time looking so smart, I was reminded of a day when I was about eleven or twelve. Mum had told me she was going to see her friend Miss Fairweather, the matron at the local nursing home. They had worked together before my brother and I were born.

'Would you like to come with me?' Mum asked. It was the school holidays and I had been twiddling my thumbs, complaining of boredom as the long days stretched ahead.

'Yes!' I jumped at the chance. I was really excited. Miss Fairweather sounded interesting; a mystical character whose name I had heard mentioned many times but who I had never met.

The following afternoon, I found myself, hand-in-hand with Mum, walking up the driveway of the nursing home. The house looked like a stately home to me, with a beautiful, manicured garden and a riot of colourful flowers lining the path. I was dressed up to the nines in my best skirt and blouse and my smart bottle-green coat. When we reached the large, dark oak door Mum tapped the heavy iron knocker. An older lady in an apron invited us in.

'Welcome,' she said, as if she had been hovering nearby, waiting for us.

I was bowled over by the smell of metallic polish and the stark, shiny wooden floor. The hallway led towards a grand, sweeping staircase, with heavy gold-framed pictures hanging on the walls.

I heard Miss Fairweather before I saw her. There was a sharp click-clack of heels and a rustle of an apron, like the wind blowing, and then she appeared. She was so regal, like the Queen! Her navy and white uniform was stiff and starched and looked immaculate. Perched on the top of her head was a toothpaste-white hat and not a strand of hair was out of place.

She looked very austere and stern, but when she smiled, her face opened up.

'Vi, how are you?' she asked, kissing Mum warmly on both cheeks.

'Good to meet you, Susan,' she said, offering her smooth hand for me to shake. I felt very grown up.

'Let's go to my office where we can have some tea,' she said, and ushered us into a room just off the hallway. There was no sign of any patients.

Mum and Miss Fairweather lapsed into easy conversation about mutual friends they had met during their nursing years and about life in the convalescent home, where many of the elderly patients came for a few months to recover from falls and various illnesses. Families took care of their elderly relatives in those days and there was a big emphasis on getting better. While they talked, the lady in the apron served us tea in bone china cups, poured from a silver teapot, before offering us cucumber and cheese sandwiches with the crusts cut off.

As I chewed as quietly as I could, I scanned the room. Huge books lined the shelves and a great mahogany desk that smelt of leather and furniture polish sat grandly towards the back.

It felt so special there, so mysterious and orderly. I asked myself a question: Did I want to be a nurse? Oh yes, I did.

Here I was: I had made it. Not only did I get to wear a smart uniform, but I now had my own ward to run as well. I knew that due to the nature of care at GOSH, I had a big job ahead of me. I found myself looking back on my time as a nurse, and it felt like only months ago that I had been a student, boiling bedpans and flooding the sluice. Now I was in charge of a whole ward, mentoring student nurses of my own. Everything felt so new. There were lots of familiar faces around, like Joan's, and staff that I knew from my previous stint at GOSH. However, the hospital employed hundreds of people and days would go by without seeing any of my friends at work. We were often on different shifts and would rarely pass each other in the corridors or in the canteen. I was constantly shaking hands with new faces, especially students who rotated around the hospital during their training, as I had done just a few years earlier.

Cohen Ward was on the ground floor on the CD side of the hospital and had a ten-bedded isolation ward for patients with infectious diseases. The other side, D side, had four cubicles and six beds in a bay for neurological patients with chronic conditions such as epilepsy, degenerative brain disease such as Batten disease, muscular dystrophy and unexplained delayed developmental milestones, where children weren't performing skills or age-specific tasks in the normal age range; also for oncology and haematology patients with leukaemia, tumours and other blood disorders.

There was a sluice and a kitchen, a treatment room on either side and a playroom on D side. There were at least two nurses assigned to each side of the ward at all times and they could call for help with an emergency bell if there were any problems.

Often I would put up extra beds for patients when these were needed. There was no system of bed management in those days and I took the view that if there was a case for a bed, then the child must have it. I was often told off for this by senior management, but it was very hard to say no. Also, there was very little parent accommodation, and sometimes parents would have to sleep on the Z-Beds that we would store in the waiting room outside the ward during the day. This made life difficult for the night nurses who had to clamber over the beds to administer treatment; the health and safety personnel of today would have been horrified. There are none of the strict rules there are today; small babies would go home in a basket on the backseat, or on their mother's lap. I recall one of my friends telling me that in order to get her wakeful newborn off to sleep, she would sling her in the back of the car in her Moses basket and go for a speedy drive around the local roads.

I would come on duty at 7.30 a.m. most days, or earlier if we were very busy, and take a report from the night nurses along with the other day nurses. After quickly touring the ward on both sides to see if all was well, and asking the nurses to clarify things if necessary, I then allocated nurses to patients and sent them to take over from the respective night nurses. If there was a child who was 'specialled' because they were especially sick or needed very special care, I would talk to the individual nurse and check the patient as often as possible. The staff nurses would ensure that there were no outstanding drugs or treatments to be give, and ensure that all intravenous drips were running according to the instructions on treatment charts.

The ward round usually began at 9 a.m., but Dr Bill Marshall, the consultant in infectious diseases, would often arrive earlier and start firing questions at me with both cylinders. He was an Australian with a very dry sense of humour and liked to call a spade a spade. He and I had a love–hate relationship. We got on very well really, but he loved to irritate me by trying to catch the nurses out. He also gave the doctors a hard time and we would all run round like headless chickens in preparation for his arrival. One of his favourite lines was, 'Have you read such-and-such in the latest *BMJ* (*British Medical Journal*)?' (or in *The Lancet*), when it would only have come out that morning, so no one could possibly have read it. He certainly kept us on our toes!

As my first Christmas on Cohen Ward approached, I decided that it was time for a ward night out. The younger nurses worked so hard and I felt it would be good for morale to take them for a few drinks. It was usual for consultants to be very generous with their staff so I mentioned my idea to Dr Marshall.

'Would you like to contribute to our night out? Buy us the first round of drinks, say?' I asked him.

'No, thanks, I wouldn't,' he replied, deadpan.

'Really? That's a shame,' I said with a smile in my voice. 'It is Christmas after all.'

He reluctantly put his hand in his pocket and threw a handful of notes and coins on to the table with a sigh.

'Thanks. This'll be enough,' I said, picking up a red fifty-pound note and walking off, leaving him to gather up his loose change.

A few days later he turned up with lots of presents which he got me to wrap up, a tradition that continued while we worked together, not that I had much say in the matter.

In the pile of gifts, I glimpsed a lovely red scarf.

'This is nice,' I said, picking it up to wrap. 'Who is it for?'

'Oh, that's for you,' he said, flinging it at me.

On another occasion, Dr Marshall made himself a sandwich in the kitchen and spread what he thought was butter on the bread. It turned out to be melted vanilla ice cream.

'Are you trying to poison me?' he yelled.

'What a good idea!' I shot back.

I quite enjoyed our sparring. The only time I ever remember him obeying an order from a nurse was when we had an Australian agency nurse helping us out on the ward. One day she poked her head out of one of the cubicles without seeing Dr Marshall, who was sitting nearby.

'Hey, blue, get your fat backside off that chair and pass me a clean sheet, will you?'

The consultant obeyed without a word; it seems that one of his fellow countrywomen definitely had the touch.

However tough he was with the nurses, Dr Marshall would always explain to the children what was going on. He and the other doctors I worked with tried to make the patients and their families feel that they were the only people he was seeing that day. There was always an undercurrent of humour on the ward. While GOSH was a very serious place, we aimed to make the hospital a very welcoming place, too.

My duties ranged far and wide. I had to ensure that all care was given accurately and safely; to check that there were enough nurses for the shift; to keep parents informed of what was happening; to promote the training of nurses; to see that the ward was kept clean and that supplies did not run out; and to ensure the safety of drugs, including controlled drugs such as morphine and pethidine, given for pain relief. If a drug error occurred, I would have to investigate it and report it to the nursing officer. I also had to attend hospital meetings as necessary, representing infectious diseases, and to liaise with the doctors and alert them to the requirements of their consultants.

Occasionally I had to give hepatitis B immunoglobulin injections to staff if they had had an inoculation injury. This could occur if they accidentally punctured their skin with a needle and there was any risk of contamination from the blood or bodily fluid of a child. There were no occupational health staff to deal with such cases then, as there are today. I remember Dr Marshall coming into the ward after an inoculation injury. I took him into the treatment room and before I had even closed the door or drawn up the injection, he had his trousers down and was exposing his bottom to me.

'Doctor, please pull up your trousers until I have the injection ready!' I said.

I could hear the nurses sniggering outside and later we all had a laugh about it. Luckily Dr Marshall knew how outspoken I was and saw the funny side. No doubt he was planning how to catch me out next.

Dr Marshall was involved in rubella vaccination development and he would take blood from all the new nurses to see if they had antibodies, in order to determine whether or not they were immune to rubella. He roped me in to help him with this mammoth task. We would go over to the School of Nursing with our bag of equipment and take blood from about thirty or forty nurses at a time. However organised I was, he would always create chaos, with blood and syringes everywhere. Some of the nurses were nervous enough about having blood taken, without the place looking like some sort of bloodbath.

'She's quite nervous, Doctor,' I would tell him if a nurse was feeling squeamish.

'Lay her on the bed and I'll come and do it,' he would shout, while the poor girl looked as if she was about to keel over with the horror of it all.

'Line 'em up, Sister Macqueen!' he would say, as if he was training me up to work in the wilds of an under-developed country, with several hundred children to vaccinate before the sun went down. However, despite his idiosyncrasies he was an excellent doctor and taught me a lot about infectious diseases.

From time to time, I even had to entertain footballers because Dr Marshall was also the doctor for the Chelsea football team and treated the players when they were ill or needing medical attention.

'Be nice to them as they may give us some money!' he would bark at me. 'Make them tea and turn on that famous charm of yours.'

Things were less formal in those days. While the footballers were always very polite and agreeable, I couldn't tell you who they were or what positions they played in. The children loved to see their sporting heroes, of course, and would ask for autographs and pictures, and spend the rest of the day smiling and kicking balls around the playroom.

When, on the rare occasions I went home, I related these stories about the footballers to my brother Peter, he was only slightly envious as he supported Tottenham!

I was more interested in going to classical concerts and the cinema than to football matches, and I also enjoyed reading during my free time. My favourite books were about Albert Schweitzer, the humanitarian, theologian, missionary, organist and medical doctor, and his work in Africa, or the expeditions of Scott to the Antarctic. I found their stories fascinating; I often imagined myself on similar arduous journeys and found myself wondering what it would be like to suffer as Scott and his men did.

As time wore on, I grew more confident in my new role. I tried to be firm but fair with the nurses and students who worked under me, and, like the sisters I had worked for and respected, I demanded a lot from them. If my nurses worked hard, I made sure I praised them and made them feel at ease. I wanted them to find me approachable, so that they always felt they could ask questions or voice worries or concerns. I liked all my nurses, but there was one with whom I got on particularly well. Abelle was the senior staff nurse, a robust and sensual girl who was always laughing. She was always fun to have around and would pull my leg, saying, 'Is that so, Sister Macqueen?' I was a guest at her wedding and she has become a lifelong friend.

As ward sister, I was faced with an increasing amount of administrative work. All nursing care had to be meticulously recorded. Individual care plans were updated at every shift and when I was taking hand-over, I would ensure that everything was written down, and altered if necessary. I was a stickler for this. I used pencil on the cards so that information could be rubbed out if it changed. This would not be allowed now, as a permanent record of all revisions must be written in ink. We were one of the first wards to try out the new system as a pilot. I welcomed changes and usually volunteered to pilot anything that the hospital wanted to test.

I often found myself thinking about work while I was at home. It normally took a long conversation with one of my flatmates, relaying in exact detail what had happened that day, then a glass of wine, and often a night out, for me to wind down. Most days as I stepped through the doorway I was like a coiled spring, with patients, parents, care plans and questions racing through my mind like a constant record.

One of the more memorable patients on Cohen Ward was Tracey, who I first met after I had been working there for a couple of months. She came to the hospital's neurological department when she was a toddler because she was having fits regularly and had unexplained delayed developmental milestones. She had many tests, but to this day we haven't put a name to her condition. Parents always thought GOSH was the end of the road, so if we couldn't solve the problem, nothing could be done. The hospital had the reputation of always making a diagnosis, but this was sometimes not the case. Tracey's condition was one of those we just couldn't identify.

She came from a family of strong women and her mother, Wendy, and granny, Iris, would always accompany her to the hospital. They were 'salt of the earth' people from the East End, proper cockneys, and enjoyed making everyone laugh with their crude jokes. Wendy was extremely plump, with mounds of raven-coloured hair, and Iris was an identikit version, albeit a skinnier and slightly greying one. Tracey remained under the care of GOSH until she was sixteen and would come in and out of the hospital for help with the control of her fits and for general assessment.

When she was about six, her language grew increasingly coarse and she would swear regularly. I suspected that she had picked up the swear words at home, but the family never swore in hospital so this was only a guess.

At the age of about eight, she started to say things like 'Fuck off. Stay away from me' or 'You're a bastard'. We told her not to use 'naughty words' and she would normally just tell us to 'fuck off' again! The bad language wasn't just restricted to the nurses; the doctors and consultants were often in her line of fire as well.

I had come across this sort of behaviour before, when working with patients who had had head injuries. The areas at the front or side (temporal) of the brain are responsible for behaviour and feelings, and if they are damaged, excessive swearing is not uncommon. Once recovered, patients are often mortified to hear of their swearing, which may be completely out of character – even chaplains have been known to suffer! We put Tracey's bad language down to her degenerative brain disorder, although I did at times suspect that she knew what she was saying.

As time went on, we got more used to it and soon learnt that telling Tracey off only made matters worse. She was also very funny. I remember one day when she was about twelve and Dr Brett, her consultant – a quiet and serious man – was examining her. He wielded his patella hammer to test the reflexes in her arms and legs and then knelt down on the floor and felt her feet.

'Ohh, that's lovely. Just rub my feet some more, would

ya? I need a good massage,' she said. We were all in fits of laughter.

A few months afterwards, we were told that Prince Charles was planning to visit the hospital and had asked if there were any particular children we wished him to meet. Royal visitors were not unusual at GOSH. Of course, there were a few obvious candidates to meet His Royal Highness, but as soon as Tracey's mother, Wendy, found out, she wouldn't let the matter drop.

'Ooohh, I'd love to meet Prince Charles,' she trilled. She and Iris were like friends to us by now, so it was hard to refuse Wendy, but we were worried about Tracey's swearing.

'Okay, but what about the language?' I asked.

'No, I'll make sure of it. You have my word, she will behave,' Wendy replied.

'Well, if she can really think about what she is saying, we'll put her forward,' I agreed.

Tracey was accepted and the big day came round. As I went to meet her and Wendy at the hospital entrance, the first thing I noticed was that she was in a wheelchair with a bandage on her leg. The wheelchair wasn't unusual, she could walk a few paces if she was in the right mood, but sometimes used one for going distances. It was the bandage that concerned me.

'Tracey, what have you done?' I asked her.

'I fell out the fucking ambulance,' she said.

I wasn't best pleased to hear that she had fallen, but the swearing clearly wasn't under control either.

'She fell out the ambulance last week and has a big bruise on her ankle,' Wendy explained. 'Few weeks in the bandage and she'll be as right as rain, won't you?'

'Fucking hurts,' Tracey scowled.

Oh dear, I thought, feeling increasingly jumpy.

We dutifully filed into the main entrance of the hospital and lined up to receive Prince Charles, along with some other children and their parents, the medical directors, chief executive and chairman of the board. The prince, smart as ever in a light grey suit, was bang on time and proceeded down the line greeting everyone.

As he came closer, I thought I might stop breathing.

Wendy was hanging off one side of Tracey's wheelchair and I was on the other side. I could feel the tension in the air; Wendy was clearly terrified of what her daughter might say, too. You could tell that Tracey was excited as she was smiling and bobbing up and down, making the wheelchair rattle slightly.

As Prince Charles approached her, I swallowed nervously.

'Hello there,' he said, bending down so he was at Tracey's eye-level. 'Oh dear, what have you done to your ankle?'

It was as if time stood still for a good few seconds. I didn't dare exhale.

'I fell out the ambulance,' she replied, straight as anything.

'I hope it heals soon. I'm sure it will. Lovely to meet you.'

He moved on and I caught Wendy's eye. She wiped the beads of cold sweat from her brow and gave me a wink.

After Prince Charles had left the hospital, we milled around in the entrance waiting for the car to take Tracey and Wendy home. Such was our relief that we couldn't stop smiling.

'You did so well, Tracey. Well done!' I told her.

'That's my girl!' Wendy added.

'I didn't fucking swear,' Tracey said.

It was at that moment that I realised she knew exactly what she was saying. Sometimes children are so much more complex than adults give them credit for. They never, ever fail to surprise me.

As Tracey and Wendy went on their way home and I walked back to the ward, I couldn't help laughing to myself. What a day!

It had been well drummed into us not to get too emotionally involved with our patients, but there were times when parents would invite us out and refuse to take no for an answer. Tracey's family was equally persuasive. Each year they invited Dr Brett, Abelle and myself to her birthday party at their home, and every year we found some excuse not to go. Normally we'd say that we were at work or had 'other commitments'.

However, on Tracey's fifteenth birthday Wendy was planning a huge party for all their family and friends, and she and Iris wouldn't take no for an answer.

'It's a special one, Sister,' Wendy pleaded. 'C'mon, we'd love to 'ave you. It wouldn't be the same if you weren't there.'

We decided we had to do the deed and I went out to buy a present for Tracey and a bunch of flowers for her mum, out of ward funds. On the day, we piled into a taxi and were driven to Tracey's local church hall where the big East End party was taking place. None of us was familiar with this part of London and as we passed the huge housing estates and terraces, I know we were all thinking that we would rather be at home enjoying our day off.

As we pulled up outside, Dr Brett turned to me. 'You

go first,' he said nervously. 'We won't stay long. Just show our faces, then we'll slip away.'

Dr Brett was such a cultured and serious person that this really was not his scene, but I admired him for coming.

We opened the door gingerly and caught Wendy's eye.

'Ahhhhh, you're here!' She let out a high-pitched scream and ran over to greet us. 'Look, Mum, they came. They're here. Oh Doctor, am I pleased to see you!'

I don't believe Wendy thought we were coming. She hugged Abelle and me and then launched herself at Dr Brett who looked positively terrified. We were well and truly in.

She then dragged us round the hall, introducing us to all her friends and relatives who kept saying how wonderful we were and how much we had done for Tracey. I felt quite embarrassed, as did Dr Brett, who kept emitting small, nervous laughs.

There were balloons and streamers everywhere and children running around screaming, obviously enjoying themselves. The music was pounding and a few adults were dancing. Drinks and party food were placed in front of us and everyone included us in their chatter about the local neighbourhood.

Then a lady went up on the small stage with a microphone.

Oh no, not karaoke, I thought. This was most definitely our cue to leave. I glanced over to Abelle and Dr Brett, who were clearly thinking the same thing.

After the lady had finished a very poor rendition of a Fleetwood Mac song, Tracey went up to the microphone.

'Will you sing?' she asked, looking directly at me. 'Go on . . .'

I must have flushed beetroot red, as a hundred or so pairs of eyes turned towards me, expecting a rendition of the latest Prince or Duran Duran number. There are many things that I can do, but holding a tune is not one of them; I am as flat as anything. I looked at Dr Brett for a way out but he just seemed relieved that Tracey hadn't picked on him. Abelle merely shrugged her shoulders.

The crowd looked on expectantly as I skirted through the chairs and made my way up to the stage.

Thinking on my feet, I grabbed the microphone and started speaking.

'Hello everyone. My name is Susan Macqueen and I work at Great Ormond Street Hospital where Tracey has been visiting for a number of years now. Thank you for inviting the three of us here today and for being so kind ...'

I went on to say a bit about the hospital and its work and as I finished and walked off the stage, there was a roar of applause and even a standing ovation. My little speech had obviously gone down well and, more importantly, I had managed to squeeze out of that tight hole. We left soon afterwards, with Dr Brett virtually sprinting to the door, but Wendy was so grateful and proud that we had come.

For every happy story during my time as ward sister, sadly there was a tragic one. In Hollywood films, everyone always gets better when they go into hospital, but this isn't always the case. Three-year-old Mary spent some time on Cohen Ward after being transferred to GOSH for tests. Her parents knew that her illness was serious because the referring hospital had suggested the possibility of leukaemia. Mary was an only child and her parents doted on her.

It was a weekday morning, just before the ward round, and Mary's mother, Kate, was already at her bedside, having spent every night at the hospital since her daughter's admission. We both knew that the doctors were going to give her the results that day.

As soon as I stepped on duty at 7.30 a.m., Kate rushed over, almost skidding across the hard floor. 'Do you know the results, Susan?' I tried to remain passive but it must have shown on my face. How could I lie to her?

'The doctor will talk to you when he comes round. It won't be long.'

'Is it leukaemia?'

Her head was cocked awkwardly to one side and her eyes bored into me. I felt cornered. I couldn't lie, not about something so important, yet it wasn't my job to break the dreadful news.

'The doctor is coming soon; he will be able to answer you,' I replied.

'It is, isn't it?'

I had no choice. I nodded twice, slowly. This is a situation I wouldn't have known how to handle earlier in my career, but as I was growing more confident I knew it was the right thing not to lie to her. Kate let out a pitiful mewing sound, followed by an ear-shattering scream, turned on her heels and ran.

I swallowed the large awkward lump that had wedged itself in my throat like a billiard ball. I took a deep breath, checked that Abelle had control of everything on the ward, and went in search of her.

I found Kate crying on the worn bench outside the main entrance of the hospital. Cigarette butts were scattered over the ground; others had obviously been there before her. It was a clear day and the sun was shining brightly, but I could see goosebumps on her arms. She was shaking. I sat down beside her and put my arm around her and squeezed gently. 'I'm so sorry,' I said. I offered to bring her a cup of tea. Who knows why anyone thinks tea is the answer to everything, but she accepted gratefully and I went back to the ward. The cleaner, Mrs Green, offered to make it and take it down to Kate. She was a robust woman, shy but friendly, always in the background mopping floors, cleaning and polishing, a quizzical expression on her face as if she had led a hundred different lives. As well as being able to see dust a few metres away, she also had an uncanny knack of appearing when most needed. She got on well with Dr Marshall and worshipped the floor he walked on.

Later, we sat in the office, by which time I had told the two doctors on duty what had happened so that they would know how to talk to Mary's parents. They went on to explain to Kate and her husband the diagnosis, treatment and prognosis, which was not good. Roger, a nervous, quiet man who avoided eye contact, sat and listened, grey-faced and with clasped hands, trying to take it in. After the doctors had left, I sat with them quietly as Kate snuffled into a tissue and Roger stared into the distance, shell-shocked and blank. 'We can go over it again,' I said. 'You may have more questions. Ask me anything you want and I'll try and answer them for you.'

Six months later, I was looking after Mary again. She stayed in the care of the hospital for some time and had most of her chemotherapy at GOSH and in the outpatients department. These would be her last days here – she was dying. I looked at the large white clock on the wall behind the bed in the cubicle. Its face stared back at me, the long, spindly metal hands clicking past stubbornly. It was eleven o'clock in the morning and I knew this was going to be one of those days ... A sad day.

The disease control had relapsed recently, and Mary's bone marrow had been overrun with diseased white cells; the outcome had been discussed with both her parents. Her father, Roger, found it very hard to come to the hospital, but Kate was always at her daughter's bedside. Why is it usually the women who have to cope with these situations? I wondered. I saw many men retreat into themselves during harrowing times. We are all children really and need those closest to us for a cuddle, a shoulder to cry on, or, even just to be there, at our side. I felt for Kate, being here alone, but didn't know the circumstances. Perhaps Roger couldn't get away from work.

I sat with Kate, listening to her fears. Days like this never got any easier to handle, but I knew I must be strong and practical: two qualities I prided myself on possessing. People have said that I always remain calm in a crisis but now I had to steel myself to cope with my emotions. Kate knew her child was dying, but didn't know what to expect. What would happen? Would she feel anything? What could she do? Mary lay before us, semi-conscious; her blonde hair splayed across the pillow and from a distance she looked almost perfect, like a china doll. But as you got closer you realised she was very sick. She was ghostly pale and her fingertips were tinged with blue. Her breath smelt of pear drops and nail varnish and her lips were cracked, despite our attempts to moisten them with Vaseline. She had a needle in her arm and a blood transfusion was running through her veins. Her breathing was very slow and laboured; she had deteriorated quite considerably since I had last seen her a few days before. I was unsuccessful at attempting to increase the rate of transfusion and thought it was futile to continue. Surely Mary would rather be with her mother, having a cuddle?

'Would you like to hold her?' I asked.

'I don't know what to do,' she stuttered.

I turned off the machine, put a blanket on her lap and lifted Mary gently into her mother's arms. Kate froze but I continued to wrap Mary up, placing Kate's arms tenderly around her.

'Mary would love a cuddle and you can make her most comfortable,' I told her.

I saw the tension run out of Kate's shoulders as she kissed her daughter's tiny cheek. Kate recoiled as her hand brushed the tubes that ran into Mary's arm; they were clearly making her anxious, so I removed the needle and put a pressure bandage over the vein, as Mary was prone to bleeding. Then I applied gentle pressure to encourage the wound to clot. Mary sighed and snuggled into her mother's breast. Both looked more settled. I instinctively knew this was the right thing to do.

'I'm just going into the next room to get rid of this equipment,' I said.

Kate looked up, wide-eyed and fearful. 'I'll only be five minutes,' I told her, placing the emergency bell by her hand.

When I returned moments later the atmosphere was quietly calm and I felt that, when medical science can't do any more, everybody should be allowed to die like this. The clock ticked in the background and sometimes I wished I could make it stop for just a few minutes more.

'Do you want anything? A cup of tea? Have you eaten?' I asked.

Parents often forgot to eat because they were so anxious. I was always reminding them that they must keep up their strength in order to support their sick children and their siblings.

Now that I was back on the ward, I could see that Mary had deteriorated further. Her breathing was erratic and slow and she had lost the last bit of colour in her face.

It hadn't worked. The hospital had done everything it could and explored every avenue available. Some days when children passed away, it made me question everything. But I knew I must keep up a certain emotional barrier, otherwise I just wouldn't be able to function; I wouldn't be able to do my job or be there for the parents. I told the nurse who was with them to take a break. I would stay. Kate clutched her daughter tightly now, as if she would never let go; they were a unit. Mary's eyes were closed and Kate was looking down at her, rocking her gently from side to side. I could see her lips moving but she was barely audible.

They were at peace.

Fourteen months later, I was on the ward going about my daily duties when, at the entrance, I saw a familiar face. It was Kate. Her dark hair was shorter, cut into a bob, and her face was rounder and rosier. She looked really well.

'Kate!'

We hugged each other warmly.

'I came to find you, Susan. I've looked all over!'

'Well, I'm always here,' I said with a laugh. 'How are you?'

'Pregnant!' she exclaimed. 'Thirteen weeks. I came to talk to the doctor about the possibility of the baby having problems. He seems to think we are in the clear. Fingers crossed.'

'Congratulations.' I was thrilled for her. 'How wonderful for you and Roger.' Despite my daily interaction with hosts of parents I do have an uncanny knack for remembering names; Roger's rolled off my tongue without me giving it a second thought.

Kate looked around the ward and at the children, some lying on their beds and others playing nearby, and lost some of her composure.

'It feels strange being back here,' she said, her eyes welling up. 'After Mary, well ... I didn't see how life would ever continue ...'

Then she stopped and looked me straight in the eye.

'I just want to say to you – you know when you made me cuddle Mary, I'm really glad you did that.'

I've grown to realise that sometimes a small gesture can make a difference. Sometimes it doesn't, but I'm glad that this time it did.

# 9

# Special Times

It wasn't just children from the UK that we treated at GOSH. Sometimes babies who had very special needs or unexplained illnesses would be flown in from other countries to be treated by us. During my second year as sister on Cohen Ward, a baby was flown in from Zambia where he lived with his British parents and two older brothers.

Steven was two months old and he had had a severe bout of gastro-enteritis. It was common in babies there, but the illness had left him unable to absorb any nutrients and he was seriously ill. He arrived in an ambulance, looking very thin and malnourished, with pale, greying skin. He had absolutely no fat on him and was like a little skeleton covered in skin, with curious, wide hazel eyes which followed everyone around the room.

His mother, Pam, was short and slight, with ash-blonde hair and a deep mahogany tan, and she spoke with a heavy South African accent. She was exhausted after the long flight and, understandably, was very anxious about Steven. Despite it being a warm summer's day, she was wearing a thick jacket.

Steven was admitted to the isolation unit and the doctor was called to take his history and examine him. His weight was well below the first percentile on the chart that marks average babies' weight.

An intravenous drip was set up and he was given clear fluids as he still had watery diarrhoea and was a little dehydrated. We noted that he was happy to take feeds by mouth, sucking eagerly on his plastic dummy. However, he was not absorbing the nutrients via his tummy, so various blood and stool tests were taken. Pam was in time for lunch so, after I had made sure she had had something to eat, we set up a Z-Bed for her in the waiting room.

'We'll look after Steven. You must try and get some sleep,' I told her. 'You can rest here. You must be shattered.'

'Thank you,' she replied. 'I'm very tired, but I'm just so relieved we are finally here. That flight seemed so slow and the last few weeks have seemed like forever. I have cried so much I think I could've filled a lake.' She tried to summon a smile.

'I'm sure. Steven's having the best care now, so try to relax if you can. I'll come and get you if we need you for any reason.'

Five minutes after I had left Pam to settle down, I peered through the waiting room door and saw that she was out for the count, fully clothed under the covers. I felt for her. One of the things I saw time and again was how tired these poor parents often were. You can never underestimate the effect of weeks of broken sleep due to a child waking, and the constant worry. More often than not, when parents reached us, they were happy to entrust their little ones to our care, never panicking about us giving the right drugs, while they finally got some much-needed rest.

After much discussion it was decided to give total parenteral nutrition (TPN) to Steven, which means introducing food into the body via a route other than the mouth, bypassing the usual process of eating and digestion.

It was decided that, under a general anaesthetic, a catheter would be inserted through his neck vein into his heart. This would enable the nutritional formula containing salts, glucose, amino acids, and so on, to be quickly distributed around his body. The process isn't without its risks, including infection, blood clots and inflammation of the gall bladder, but it was decided that this was Steven's best chance of recovering. Once the procedure was fully explained to Pam, she was in agreement and signed the consent forms. There were plenty of tears as she sat nervously waiting for Steven to come out of theatre, but the operation went smoothly.

'I wish Ned was here,' she said wistfully. Ned was Pam's husband; they owned a farm in Zambia and had two other young boys, who had already started school there. Ned was unable to come to England because he had to keep the business running and they wanted continuity for their other children. It was hard when families were split up for long periods of time, but we tried to make things as comfortable as possible for Pam. Initially, she had a bed in the waiting room, but later we found her a bed in the limited parents' accommodation on the fifth floor of the hospital. Each of the rooms contained two single beds and wardrobes, a couple of chairs and a table. Now we have a parents' hotel, which has thirty rooms with self-contained kitchens, and a lot of the cubicles at the hospital also have ensuite bathrooms and toilets, but back then it was very basic. Pam had no family or friends nearby, so this was a very difficult time for her. I made a point of trying to chat to her over a cup of tea when I wasn't too busy, as did all the staff.

In those days we made up the special intravenous feeds on the ward with a sterile technique, wearing gowns and using sterile gloves. Now it is made up in a special cabinet in the hospital pharmacy and the sterility is much better controlled. The solutions took about an hour to put together because there were many additives, such as vitamins, amino acids, antibiotics and potassium. Total parenteral nutrition was fairly new at the time and there were few commercial preparations for children; hence we had to add many components ourselves to ensure that the children received the correct nutrition for healthy growth. It took two people to check that everything was correct and introduce the solution to the giving sets. We would have as many as three patients on TPN at any one time and with other intravenous drugs to give every four or six hours, it was extremely hard work staying on top of our workload.

Using sterile towels, swabs and antiseptic solution, we then attached the giving set to the catheter in Steven's skinny neck via a very fine needle; it was hair's-breadth thin and barely visible to the naked eye. This procedure needed a lot of concentration and a very steady hand, as you could easily puncture the rubber catheter with the needle. There were no commercially available connections small enough for children in those days and nurses were well known for adapting equipment to suit the patient's needs. This would certainly not be allowed now.

I remember one day, soon after Steven had had his operation, when I was doing the connection on my own as we were short of nurses. Just at that moment the nursing officer knocked on the door of the cubicle and poked her head in.

'How many nurses do you have for tomorrow, Sister Macqueen?' she asked. 'Can you lend someone?'

I ignored her, as I was concentrating on doing the procedure.

'They are short over on the cardiac wing and I thought maybe you could spare someone?'

She wasn't taking the hint that I was not replying and my concentration was ruined. I dropped the needle on the floor.

'Curses!' I was annoyed now and Steven started squirming about, as small babies do. Luckily I had another needle, but I was anxious that the blood in the catheter should not clot.

'Please can you let me finish!' I shot back at her. 'Really! I am trying to concentrate. Can't you see that?'

'There's no need to be like that, Sister!' She turned on her heel and left in a huff.

With my mind now back fully on the job, I managed to connect the needle and catheter and the drip appeared to be working well. I didn't fancy having to tell the doctors that the catheter was blocked and we would have to insert another one, involving a second operation. This was an example of where the old system of matrons was so much better, as they were more in touch with the day-to-day life of nurses; they would never have dreamt of interrupting somebody who was doing such an intricate procedure. Nursing officers, on the other hand, were sometimes out of touch and solely focused on staffing and numbers; they often forgot, or didn't understand, the backbone of care.

Steven was weighed daily and gradually started putting on weight, although he had episodes of infection that required intravenous antibiotics and the occasional removal and replacement of his IV line. Despite our best efforts, we knew his line could be a source of infection; some of his gut bacteria leaking into his blood stream could also cause possible complications. He was not allowed anything by mouth so as to give his stomach a rest. The lining of the gut had been stripped by his previous infection and needed time to regrow.

We got to know Pam very well during this period. She missed her husband dreadfully and used to ring him from the hospital pay phone every night, without fail; it was long before the days of mobile phones and Skype. I know she felt very lonely at times, but she gradually made friends with other parents on the ward. I would increasingly see her chatting to the other mothers, especially those whose children were with us for a few weeks or longer. Parents often formed lifelong friendships in the hospital – I think perhaps because they understood each other in a way that no one else could and had similar memories of GOSH.

One night, a few months after Pam and Steven first arrived, some of us were going out for a drink after work and we invited Pam to come along. We often went to the old Victorian pub round the corner, The Lamb in Lamb's Conduit Street, where many hospital people gathered after their shifts. The pub served great beer and there was always a warm atmosphere. Pam was so grateful to be included and thoroughly enjoyed herself. It was a proper girlie night out with a lovely group of staff nurses. We all worked well together and enjoyed each other's company away from the ward. There were plenty of drinks and giggles and no mention either of the hospital or of Steven. The younger nurses entertained us with tales of their boyfriends and dates with the doctors. I guess we crossed the professional barriers by socialising with Pam that evening and this might be frowned upon today. However, I felt that empathy and compassion were needed on that occasion. I think the slice of normality did her the world of good.

Steven's care wasn't without its hiccups. The requirements for his TPN had to be worked out daily. The poor houseman would spend a long time completing the charts, while the dietician would ensure that the requirements were correct, and the pharmacist that all the drugs were compatible. I remember spending a long time each day checking Steven's TPN and additives, alongside another nurse, and putting a label on the bag which listed them all, before attaching it to his catheter.

One day I was busying myself with this when one of the staff nurses came by.

'Did you add the antibiotics?' she asked. Steven had another infection and it was crucial to his recovery for him not to develop antibiotic resistance.

'Yes,' I replied. I was sure I had; I was always very careful.

'It's wasn't on the label so we had to discard the bag and start all over again.'

I was horrified. How could I have made a mistake like that?

Luckily the night nurse had noticed, and Steven did not suffer, but that wasn't the point – even sisters make mistakes. The oversight was reported to the nursing officer, who then asked to see me. I explained what had happened and admitted that I had obviously not checked what had been written on the label closely enough. She didn't need to tell me off; I felt bad enough already. Parents had to be informed of any errors and I apologised profusely to Pam. She seemed very understanding but I vowed that I would check myself twice over in future.

Within a few months, Steven was developing well and putting on weight, and his little legs were slowly filling out. It was decided to start him on a 'chix' feed, which I had come across on the endocrine and metabolic ward earlier in my career. It is basically puréed chicken, which is easily digestible. It smelt and tasted awful but Steven enjoyed it and gobbled it down greedily. Gradually other nutrients were introduced and when he appeared to be absorbing it well, the amount of total parenteral nutrition was reduced.

Eventually, over several months, Steven was taken off TPN and the catheter was removed. As he was well past weaning age he was now eating some solids, in addition to which he had his special milk.

'Look at that tummy,' I would joke to Pam. 'Never mind putting on more weight – he needs to go on a diet at once!'

After being on Cohen Ward for eleven months, all agreed that Steven was ready to go home. Pam couldn't believe it. When the day came for them to leave, she sobbed and clutched our hands.

'I shall miss you all,' she told us. 'I can't tell you how grateful I am to you and all the doctors.'

Back in Zambia, Pam has faithfully written me a Christmas card every year since then, with a little note about Steven's progress.

When he was twenty-one, Steven decided to travel around Europe and stayed in London for a few days as part of his tour. Pam had warned me that he might come and see me, but I didn't know when it would be. I was an infection control nurse with an office in the microbiology department by then.

'Is there a Sister Macqueen working here?' The voice was that of a young man and had a distinct South African accent.

I jumped up, knowing it must be Steven.

There he stood, about five foot six inches tall, looking as healthy as any young man, with a huge grin and perfect white teeth. Obviously, he only knew me by his mother's description, but I certainly knew him. We chatted about life and his travels and I took him to see the cubicle where he had spent all those months as a baby. The only abnormality I picked up was that he was afraid of water. Neither he nor I could think why this should be, but if that was the only thing wrong then we had all done a very good job. It was lovely seeing him; I couldn't believe the twenty-one years had gone by so quickly. More recently I heard that Ned had died, leaving Pam to manage the farm with the help of Steven and his brothers. I would love to meet up with her again some time. I guess time will tell.

Two weeks after Steven and his mother returned to South Africa, a child was admitted to the isolation ward with meningococcal meningitis, a serious bacterial infection of the fluid that surrounds the brain. Left untreated, it carries a high mortality rate and swift action is the key to any child's recovery.

Richard was six years old and otherwise a healthy boy, with a shock of blond hair and a really chubby tummy. His mother, Belinda, said he had complained of feeling unwell during the day. Not only had he been unable to finish his favourite meal of fish and chips because he felt sick and had a headache, but he refused to go outside after school and play. These were the days when children played happily out in the street with their friends, the boys on their bikes and with balls, the girls with their skipping ropes, hopscotch and Cindy dolls. Computers were at least ten years away and children's television was also limited. Belinda explained that she had thought Richard might have picked up a tummy bug at school, but just before retiring to bed at around midnight she had been to his room and noticed a horrible red rash on his neck.

'I knew about meningitis,' she told us. 'I got him up to see if I could see the rash under the bathroom light but it was a struggle to wake him. I tried to take him to the toilet but he was really drowsy and kept falling all over the place. That's when I rang for the ambulance.'

She and her husband, Mr West – we never got on first-name terms – rushed him to the local hospital in Hertfordshire, where they lived. Richard was admitted immediately and had various blood tests. He was then transferred to GOSH and I met them all at around ten o'clock the following morning.

The first thing that happened was that Richard was given a lumbar puncture to collect fluid from his spine for analysis, and had various blood tests to identify his infection. He had a high temperature, was very confused and kept crying softly. We put him on an antibiotic intravenous drip even before the test results came through as prompt treatment is essential, and I made sure one of the nurses monitored him closely. By early afternoon, tests confirmed the worst: it was meningococcal meningitis.

'Nurse, what happens now? Why aren't there more doctors here?' Mr West, Richard's father, was a northerner and his tone was aggressive and demanding. He was a giant of a man, like a human bear, with colossal hairy hands with which he gesticulated as he spoke. I reasoned that his attitude was due to anxiety, having seen a number of similar cases in the past. I had developed a fairly thick skin by then and never took these outbursts to heart, although I must admit that I was quite intimidated by this man. The doctor saw him several times to explain what was happening to Richard, but he continued to challenge me.

'I want another opinion, Sister. Get another doctor here now!' he yelled, one arm waving wildly.

'That doctor's opinion will be the same. We can't predict the outcome at this stage, but the next day or two will be critical.'

'Someone must know the chances?' He was so close to me that I could practically feel the black wisps of his beard on my face. I was showered in a fine spray of spit as he spoke.

'I'm afraid not.'

He paced up and down as if his life depended on it, while Belinda sat at Richard's bedside, anxiously looking on.

Later in the day, I told Mr West I had found him a bed in the waiting room.

'Are you mad? I am not leaving this bedside!'

Belinda looked embarrassed, but didn't dare apologise on behalf of her husband.

'It will be extremely crowded in here. Abelle will have to take frequent observations and she will disturb you.' I tried to explain that a Z-Bed in the waiting room was far more practical.

'I insist. Bel can sleep there. I am waiting here.'

'Nurse, I wondered when . . .' Belinda started to speak but Mr West butted in.

'Will he be okay afterwards? Are there any after-effects?'

I decided to sit in the cubicle with both of them and answer their questions as best I could. Mr West continued to dominate the situation and I wasn't getting very far.

'Perhaps, Belinda, you could stay overnight, while Mr West, you get some rest at home? We normally only allow one parent to stay – it's just that we have such limited space here.'

'Absolutely not. I'm staying here and nothing you say will make me agree to anything else.'

It was useless trying to negotiate anything, so I let the matter drop.

Mr West remained like this throughout his son's stay. Within a week the infection cleared and Richard started to be more alert and like his old self, so we began planning his transfer back to his local hospital.

'No, we're staying here until we can go home. I'm not moving,' Mr West would say, holding his ground as if he was spoiling for a fistfight.

'Well, he's non-infectious now, so we'll need to move him to the other side of the ward. To one of the bays,' I tried to explain.

'No. Absolutely not. We're staying here.'

'But we need the bed for another child who has an infection. We don't have enough beds here, Mr West. Please try to understand.'

'Understand? What you need to understand is that I want Richard to remain here, right in this cubicle, until we go home.'

'It will be beneficial for him to mix with other children. It will help his recovery,' I continued.

'Mix with other children and their germs? No thanks.'

Again I was forced to back down.

I even asked Dr Marshall to have a word with him about the bed situation, thinking he might listen to another man. But the consultant had met his match in Mr West and was unable to persuade him to allow his son to be moved, even though we had agreed to keep Richard at GOSH when he could have been treated just as well at his local hospital.

Abelle also struggled with this difficult man and one encounter with him left her purple in the face with pent-up rage.

'Sister, he is a nightmare of gigantic proportions,' she said. 'He demands things constantly, yet won't listen if I ask him to help or to move. His poor wife can't get a word in edgeways.'

'I know. I can't understand why he is so stubborn and why he won't think of other children's needs,' I responded. 'It's infuriating, isn't it?'

'And yet Richard is such a lovely child,' Abelle continued. 'He seems to be developing normally and is recovering really well.'

'I know. It's strange. Perhaps he has the mother to thank for that.'

When the time came for Richard to leave, Mr West didn't shake my hand or say thank you to any of the other nurses or the doctors. He just marched off apace, with his son and wife trailing behind him. I felt I had failed with this father, as there must have been a reason why he was so intractable. Cases like this made me think hard about what I could have done differently, or whether I might have approached the situation in another way. They made me feel frustrated that there were still problems I was unable to solve.

As there were so many specialties in the isolation ward, we had many doctors visiting the unit. I particularly remember Dr Richard Bonham-Carter, a cardiologist who was a lovely gentleman. I had seen him on the cardiac wing when I was a student but got to know him on Cohen Ward. We had a few children with MRSA transferred there from the cardiac unit and he would visit them. He was a brilliant doctor, but very unassuming and always ready for a chat. He had the knack of making parents feel at ease and special and he also had a wonderful rapport with the children. He treated everyone the same, whether he was talking to his senior colleagues or to the ward cleaner.

With one of the leading paediatric surgeons, David Waterston, Dr Bonham-Carter developed the thoracic unit at GOSH, which was the first joint medical and surgical ward devoted entirely to the diagnosis and treatment of children with chest and heart disease. This later culminated in the Cardiac Wing opening in 1988. Their type of work in heart and lung disease was often referred to as 'fixing the plumbing', so before long Doctors Bonham-Carter and Waterston were known affectionately around the hospital as 'the plumber and his mate'. The heart and lung unit may have started as a ten-bedded ward but was proof of the two men's vision: by combining expertise and disciplines, treatment could be far more effective. The model was far ahead of its time and set the precedent for how the hospital still works today.

There were many wonderful people at GOSH and we had a great social life. I used to play squash on the hospital courts and got to know several people who have become lifelong friends. It was good fun racing around the court after work and we started a hospital league, which included doctors, nurses, technicians, dieticians and physiotherapists. Some were good players, others just beginners; I liked to think of myself as top-middle range! Afterwards, a group of us would go to The Lamb for a drink and out for a meal most weeks. I met John, who was to become my husband, around this time. John was Irish, with dark curly hair, and was very shy and quiet. He worked in the immunology department of the hospital and was often to be found nursing a pint in the pub after work. Occasionally he came to the ward to collect blood samples but he worked mainly in the hospital laboratory.

During my third year on Cohen Ward, one of the laboratory technicians paired us up for one of the fundraising balls at The Dorchester in Park Lane. The event was in aid of the National Hospital for Neurology and Neurosurgery. I had arranged to meet John there as I was working and didn't know what time I would get away. Of course I was late, having spent some time – after finally managing to hand over – changing into a long, aquamarine ball gown. By the time I arrived at the hotel, the guests were just finishing the first course of the meal. I apologised profusely to John, but I could tell by the surprised look on his face that he thought I had stood him up.

'I brought this for you,' he said, handing me a pretty white orchid he had placed on the table.

I pinned it to my dress and felt it was a sweet gesture.

After the meal, I suddenly realised that we were the only two left sitting at the table. Everyone else was dancing.

'Fancy a dance?' I asked.

'I'm not a great dancer,' he replied bashfully.

'Neither am I, come on!' I grabbed his hand and off we went.

Just like me, he couldn't do the waltz or even the quickstep, but we could both do rock-and-roll – or at least a tame version of it. We amused ourselves by observing other couples and speculating who was going out with whom and we talked briefly about the hospital and other interests we had in common, like classical and folk music and the theatre. I couldn't help smiling when he told me that he was a big fan of football and supported Arsenal.

Later in the evening, John turned to me suddenly. 'Why were you so late?' he asked.

'I'm so sorry. It was work. I struggled to get away.' I knew he had felt a bit of a lemon waiting for me and I felt bad about it afterwards because he was a decent, honest man.

As we were leaving he put me in a taxi and kissed my flushed cheek.

'I wonder whether you'd like to go out next week, to see *A Midsummer Night's Dream* at Regent's Park?' he asked.

'Yes, I'd really like that,' I replied, and a faint feeling of butterflies sat in the pit of my stomach.

We had a wonderful evening in the park. It was one of those sublime summer nights like they have on the Continent, and we sat on my picnic rug with our drinks and some food and watched the magical play.

Afterwards, when the sun had gone down, we walked through the park and John saw me home to my flat and kissed me on the doorstep. I seem to remember that I rather enjoyed it, but I was very reserved about my feelings. I didn't want to get hurt so I kept him firmly at arm's length and never gave anything away. The saying about the Irish answering a question with a question is John all over. He now confesses that he was quite in awe of me at first and saw me in my role as Sister as haughty, efficient and strict. He was as timid as a mouse about the way he felt, too.

Our friendship gradually developed as we got to know one another better, but still we mostly socialised in a large group of hospital folk. In the winter of 1974 I remember I was arranging a skiing holiday for a party of people, including John. Some of them had partners and others were single, including myself. During this time, two of the couples split up, then they were back together again, and it reached a stage when I didn't know whether to book single or double rooms, or how many of each we would need. To cut a long story short, I was left with a double room instead of two single rooms for John and me. I hadn't planned it that way, honestly! When we arrived at our destination, I nervously told him what had happened.

'That's fine,' he said, without raising any objections. Every night we fell exhausted into bed after a day on the ski slopes and I wondered whether something more might happen. John was painfully reserved, though, and I still had no inkling that he really liked me. It was only years later, when we got to know each other better, that he said I had orchestrated the room allocation on purpose. I maintain that it was a Freudian slip!

Christmas was always a special time at the hospital. During September and October a group of us would start thinking about producing the staff Christmas show. As I had no acting talent I was the producer. We would begin by putting out a message in the hospital and at the Institute of Child Health, the research arm of GOSH, asking who would like to be in it, or to help, and in those days there was no shortage of helpers. We would meet regularly, when work permitted, to sort out the scripts, programme and rehearsal dates. Freddie, a music teacher who drank in The Lamb and lived locally, always offered to play the piano and was the best talent we had. We made all our own props and costumes or begged and borrowed them. Nothing was out of bounds. I once remember summoning the courage to ask a consultant orthopaedic surgeon if he had a spare quilted smoking jacket we could borrow.

'Which one would you like? I have several. A purple one, a black one, a grey one – take your pick!' he replied.

Rehearsals were chaotic and there were always several key people missing because they were working. We insisted that everyone must attend the dress rehearsal just before the show, but we never even achieved this – it was very much a case of 'It'll be alright on the night!' We rehearsed and performed in the basement of the School of Nursing, on the corner of Lamb's Conduit Street and Great Ormond Street, where our various colourful and very amateur props were stored in a dusty cupboard. Our evenings would be spent haphazardly sewing costumes, painting background scenery and protesting loudly that the words were incorrect or the acting not up to standard. The singers would be croaking away while we would be arguing about how things should be done. To say that rehearsals were a shambles was an understatement. My staff nurses on the ward would instinctively know that I found it hard to concentrate on anything else while the show was going on.

'Are we in a bad mood today, Sister?' Abelle would ask, sensing that I was grumpy. 'Anything on your mind?'

On the day of the show she would tease me and ask, 'Doing anything special tonight, Sister?'

One of the highlights was the consultants' sketch. By about the end of November they would start asking, 'Will I get a part? I haven't received my invitation yet!' It was an event eagerly anticipated by everyone, doctors and staff alike.

The sketch was a top secret affair, because the various consultants it had been written for would only be given their parts on the night, along with their costumes. This made it all the more exciting because it was too late by then for them to argue with what had been written! We performed the show for two nights to begin with, then extended it to three as the years went by. The tickets were priced at £2.00 and we always sold out. The first night was usually also the first proper dress rehearsal and wasn't without its mishaps. The basement, where the show was held, had one aisle down the middle, with chairs on both sides and standing room along the edges. The air would be foggy with smoke and sweat, and invariably the room would get far too hot as people came in from the cold wrapped in sweaters and coats. Many people had been to The Lamb and sunk a few drinks before the show started and no one ever held back. John always came with his friends and they joined in the heckling with the rest of the jovial crowd.

The room opposite the corridor leading to the 'theatre' was the dressing room and although the artistes were told to keep their voices down, they kept forgetting and often didn't know when it was their turn to go onstage. The cast had to change their costumes so quickly between scenes that modesty went out of the window. I remember the time when one of my colleagues stripped off completely. I grabbed a long skirt to protect her modesty, only to find I had framed her in the opening of her skirt for all the audience to see. All the while, I just kept yelling, 'Next act on stage!' The adrenalin never stopped flowing during the show but we all loved it.

During the interval on the last night, the relevant consultants were invited backstage. They were all given a drink before being helped into their costumes and finally shown their scripts. Some of the men were reluctant to remove their trousers, but we soon cured that with a few stern words and a glass of wine. After they had all asked questions about their roles, we were ready to begin. The voice-over on the loud speaker would announce the title of the opening scene and the audience would be so silent you could hear a pin drop. Everyone was relishing the prospect of seeing the hospital's senior and most respected members of staff dressed up as Aladdin, Tinkerbell or the Ugly Sisters. The fairy story would open with the consultants throwing themselves into their acting roles, or at least giving it their best shot. There were shrieks of laughter from the audience when performers were recognised and boos at all the jokes. The consultants themselves often looked equally horrified but tradition dictated that they just kept going. The singing was usually painfully out of tune but occasionally a consultant had a top-notch singing voice and he would get a roaring encore.

One year we did Snow White and the Seven Dwarfs

with Dr Marshall as one of the dwarfs. As part of the sketch, he had to perform 'The Dance of the Seven Veils'. I had dressed him in various flowing scarves for this and he was wearing full make-up, including some nice pink lipstick. My job was to push him onstage in a wicker laundry basket from which he would rise and do his exotic dance. I bundled his head down into the basket and closed the lid and just as I was wheeling him onstage he yelled out, 'I've got cramp, I've got cramp. Let me out, woman!' Of course the audience heard and started to laugh. I went on pressing the lid down, partly on purpose, and he continued struggling to escape. Eventually he did limp out of the basket, clutching his calf, but it just made the sketch all the funnier.

After the show we had a party in the doctors' mess and it was always the party of the year, going on until the early hours of the morning. I remember one nurse being in such a poor way after drinking too much that I didn't like to leave her. In the end I took her to Casualty at University College Hospital where they kept her in overnight. She wasn't happy when she came to and realised she was in the company of a number of other inebriated people.

Christmas for the children was always a big affair. Preparations would start well in advance and the wards would be decorated by the play leaders – with help from the children – with tinsel and paper-chains hanging from the windows and doors. In each ward we had a cosy corner, usually the playroom, for food, drink and relaxing as we all did double shifts at Christmas. Parents could come in and help themselves to refreshments, as we wanted to make it as enjoyable as possible for them.

The theatre staff and the surgeons were usually

dressed up as fairies and elves or reindeer, and we disguised a trolley as a sleigh, on which had been placed a huge sack of presents for the children and their visiting siblings.

On Christmas Eve, the nurses would turn their cloaks inside out to display the red lining and sing carols in the stairwell of the wards. The strains of 'Silent Night' and 'Away in a Manger' would echo around the wards and sound quite haunting. Afterwards, the nurses would walk around and sing a couple of carols in each ward. I remember feeling slightly homesick at these times, which was unusual for me, and I always called Peter, and then Mum and Dad, to tell them I was thinking of them. When I was Sister of Cohen Ward, I did not get Christmas off for about eight years. At that point I went home to Cambridge only about once or twice a year but kept in touch with my parents by telephone. I enjoyed their occasional visits to London when we would all go sightseeing.

In the late hours of Christmas Eve, a group of nurses, wearing their uniforms, would go down to Covent Garden market to pick up some bargains, such as fruit, vegetables, flowers and nuts. The market people were always very generous and we came back laden with an abundance of delights for the big day.

When the children woke, Santa Claus, who was often one of the medical registrars, bearded and dressed in a red costume, would go round the ward handing out presents. He wouldn't accept a drink because he was normally on duty, but all the nurses would get a kiss from him before he continued on his rounds.

We would tuck into turkey, roast potatoes and all the trimmings, followed by Christmas pudding with brandy butter, and everyone would eat it sitting around a table or on their children's beds. This is no longer allowed for health and safety reasons.

Early on Christmas Day, a film crew was often to be seen around the hospital. This was because of a television programme, hosted by Tony Blackburn or Noel Edmonds, which went out live on the BBC. They would roam around the wards talking to the children about what was wrong with them and to the staff and parents about the care they were receiving. I would often record the programme on my VHS video player and watch it when I returned home late that night. It always made me feel choked up and I often shed a few tears, even though I worked there. There was a real feeling of togetherness in the hospital, despite all the illness, and this programme always reminded me that I was working somewhere very special indeed. All in all, I have very fond memories of the festive seasons on Cohen Ward.

## 10

# Fundraising Fun in Abu Dhabi

From its earliest days the hospital has relied on donations to continue its work. Long before the advent of the NHS in 1948, fund-raising was necessary to subsidise the care and treatment of every patient and pay the staff's salaries. Nowadays, even though basic provisions are financed by the state, gifts from celebrities and major companies, in addition to the proceeds of fund-raising, allow the hospital to remain a world leader in childhood medicine. The money helps to build state-of-the-art facilities, develop new treatments, provide the best equipment, and support patients and their families. Nowadays there is a huge variety of initiatives to help raise the £50 million that is needed annually, including sponsored sporting activities like trekking all over the world and skydiving.

In 1975, I heard about the opportunity to do some fund-raising in Abu Dhabi. In this case, a group of generous expats had asked for a patient and a nurse to fly out to receive a cheque for the hospital. A patient was chosen from the plastics' ward and I volunteered to go with her. Her name was Rosie and she had Apert syndrome, which is a congenital disorder where the skull bones fuse abnormally, the eyes protrude, there is webbing of the hands and feet, and also hearing loss. Rosie was seventeen years old and had been operated on numerous times to help prevent a build-up of pressure on the brain. Not having met her before, I arranged to get to know Rosie and her parents at the hospital one day after my shift. When we met, I could see that, despite much craniofacial surgery, Rosie still had abnormal facial features; otherwise she was a typical teenager. She was fairly tall with long, wavy dark-blonde hair. She had a very outgoing personality, full of sparkle, and coped with her disfigurement admirably.

'People can stare all they like. I don't care,' she said, and 'I'm beautiful inside as well as out.'

Rosie wore a hearing aid but could lip-read very well. I made sure I was facing her when I spoke and that I mouthed my words clearly but not necessarily slowly. After five minutes in her spritely company, I knew we would get on well during our holiday in the sun. Rosie's mother was planning to accompany her but when the time came she was unable to fly, due to an ear infection, so her father, Alan, came instead. I joked that we had to keep up the standards of glamour expected of those representing GOSH, with at least three changes of clothes a day, as we would be meeting the ambassador and many other interesting people. I'm sure Alan wondered what he was letting himself in for, but he had a good sense of humour and laughed along, saying, 'Girls, eh – I just don't get it!'

We met at Heathrow, heaved our luggage on to a trolley and caught the overnight flight, sadly only in economy class. We had quipped that we fancied seats in first class, with glasses of ice-cold champagne or freshly squeezed orange juice and a bowl of cashew nuts, but it was not to be. I said that I was sure there would be plenty of luxury to come later in our trip.

We landed in Dubai in the early morning after a

seven-hour flight and were taken by car to the hotel. We had left the dreary autumn weather behind in London and arrived in glorious sunshine. Off came our winter boots and on went our sparkly sandals. The hotel staff gave us a warm welcome and we were allocated their best rooms, with huge beds, a mountain of pillows, luxurious ensuite bathrooms, complete with robes and fluffy slippers, and balconies overlooking the sea. Rosie and her dad's double rooms had a connecting door. Rosie made me laugh with some of her teenager-isms. 'This is the best hotel, like, EVER!' she said repeatedly.

As we had had breakfast on the plane we decided to try to get some sleep, as our first appointment was not until 1 p.m. I set my alarm as I was anxious not to oversleep – it wouldn't make a good impression. I woke much refreshed and after checking that Alan and Rosie were on their way, I put on a lightweight dress. Alan was waiting for me in the grand foyer. Ten minutes later Rosie appeared, looking super-glamorous and bursting with excitement about the day ahead.

'We can't keep the photographers and the ambassador waiting,' I said, pretending to be cross with her.

The car took us to the expats' club where a fund-raising event was under way. We walked in and were immediately greeted by a number of people, then introduced to the ambassador. He was a short, jolly man who did not have any airs or graces and was much respected in the local community. Rosie was the centre of attention and she was in her element. After about five minutes in her company it was as if she didn't have a disfigurement at all. I was then coaxed into playing a game of darts with the ambassador to raise the stakes. It wasn't my best game but I managed a bullseye on the second round and there were many cheers because no one had yet managed to beat the ambassador; it was a total fluke! I lost the game well and truly after that, but it was a good laugh. We were given drinks and food and people crowded round asking questions about the hospital. GOSH is known around the world and they were very interested in our work. Rosie told them what a wonderful place it was and about her treatment, which had included one ten-hour operation and many smaller ones to help correct her skull. She admitted that she had had no idea how big the hospital was or about its ambitious fund-raising activities. Alan appeared to be enjoying himself, too, and sang the praises of the surgeons and nurses who had looked after his daughter.

Back at the hotel, I thought we really ought to have another rest. It was early evening by then and we had another full day tomorrow. However, Rosie was so full of beans that I suggested cocktails by the pool. Alan looked at me as if I was a bit mad, but I was determined to make it a trip for both of them to remember and played along with the glamorous lifestyle.

'Get your swimwear on and I'll meet you in five minutes by the pool,' I said, winking at Rosie. A few minutes later I was sitting on a sun lounger, towel in hand, waiting for them – I had a reputation to live up to, after all. They soon appeared, Rosie in a bikini and robe and Alan in his shorts and shirt. Rosie and I went for a swim while Alan watched us as we bobbed up and down in the setting sun. I then enticed her to the swim-up cocktail bar by the side of the pool. Here we sat on stone seats in the water and ordered fruit cocktails with all the trimmings, which Rosie kept saying was 'so cool'. Her father wanted to know what was in it and I gave him a look. I hoped he trusted me.

'This is an Abu Dhabi special, Alan. Would you like one?'

I ordered another and I could see his face relax when he realised that the drink was non-alcoholic.

We all slept well that night and had agreed to meet for an early breakfast, as we were being picked up first thing to be taken on a tour of the city. The day starts early in Dubai because of the heat. Guess who was late? Rosie, who I must admit appeared looking tired.

The high point of our tour was lunch in a very smart restaurant at the top of a really tall and ornate building. We were ushered into the lift and when we stepped out, there was this fantastic view of the city and beach. While we ate our meal, the building was gradually rotating, but the movement was barely perceptible. The afternoon was to be taken up with the presentation of the cheque, which was the object of our visit, and I knew Betty Barchard, our chief nurse, would be there. She had flown out earlier to attend a meeting in Oman and lay the foundations for work in the Middle East.

Once again we dressed up in our glad rags – I had emphasised to Rosie that we couldn't be seen in the same clothes twice – and were driven to another hotel where the reception was being held. Betty greeted us all with open arms and introduced us to everyone. She was a tall, chic, red-headed lady who loved entertaining and the high life; she would go out of her way to include nurses in the more glamorous side of health care. The formal speeches over, Betty gave a talk about the hospital. Then Rosie was asked to come and receive the cheque and say a few words.

She cleared her throat and took the microphone.

'Hi everyone. My name is Rosie and I've been a patient at Great Ormond Street for nearly seventeen years. I have a condition called Apert syndrome, which is a genetic abnormality, meaning that it causes abnormalities in the formation of my skull and other parts of my body. I have had ten operations to correct the problems and help me grow as normally as possible. This means I've been to departments all over the hospital, such as plastic surgery, neurology, speech therapy, physiotherapy, orthodontic and audiology, where they have helped me with lots of things. Everyone is so lovely and always trying to make me laugh. The only thing they are not very good at is putting on bandages – they are always falling off! I have to tell the nurses how to do it properly.'

'I go to a normal school and I'm really happy there. I have lots of friends and really want to be a nurse when I leave. I think I have the staff at Great Ormond Street to thank for that.'

She was a total star. I looked around and many people had tears in their eyes. You would think Rosie was born to do public speaking and I felt very humble in her presence. We couldn't have chosen a better patient to represent the hospital.

The following day we flew home after an exhausting, exciting time. When I said goodbye to Alan and Rosie at Heathrow, I knew they had both loved every minute of it. I eventually lost touch with the family but I often think of Rosie's knowing personality, thanks to her parents, and the fact that it would always help her to overcome any problems and see her through life.

I still saw John in The Lamb after work and during our squash tournaments, and my stomach always did a somersault when we met. The following week, he came up to the ward with some fresh doughnuts from the Holborn Bakery in Lamb's Conduit Street.

'Sue, I bought these for you and the others,' he said timidly, passing them over in a paper bag.

'Thank you.'

He was such a polite and thoughtful chap. By that point I knew I really liked him, but still felt embarrassed about showing my emotions. I knew he enjoyed folk music, as I did, and I had bought two tickets for a concert with the intention of seeing if he would come with me.

'Fancy coming to see Bob Davenport with me later this week?' I asked. 'He's playing in Islington. The gig is on Wednesday.'

'Oh yes, sounds great. Anyway, must get back to work,' he said and disappeared.

'Doughnuts for us,' Abelle joked. 'I can't imagine why he would want to bring them up here.'

It was a fabulous gig, followed by supper, and he continued to bring treats up to the ward every week or so. I knew I was falling for him, but I didn't want anyone to know, especially John.


Not long after my return from Abu Dhabi, I came across my first case of Crouzon syndrome, another inherited genetic condition that causes an unusual facial appearance. This syndrome affects fifteen in every million babies. Although brain development is normal, it causes craniosynostosis, which is where the flat plates of bone that form the skull fuse together early in life, interfering with the growth of the skull and distorting the shape of the head. Other characteristics of the syndrome are a high, prominent forehead, a beak-shaped nose and abnormalities of the eyes. Common problems include damage to the optic nerve, deafness, obstruction of the airways and learning disabilities.

Lucy was transferred to Cohen Ward from the neurosurgical ward as she had a viral infection and a rash. She was four months old and had had a tracheostomy because she was suffering from tracheomalacia. This means that the trachea is not properly developed: instead of being rigid, the walls are floppy. As the trachea is the first part of the windpipe, breathing difficulties begin soon after birth and Lucy had been in hospital ever since.

'It has been a living hell,' her mother told me when we met. I did feel for Lucy's poor parents, who had two other perfectly healthy children at home and were very good-looking people. It must have been a shock to have a baby that looked so different. Congenital tracheomalacia is very rare and it was a condition a number of staff hadn't seen before.

Lucy was put in the end cubicle and had a nurse with her all the time. We had been warned about her eyes and the risk of them popping out of their shallow sockets because they were too small. Sometimes, in such cases, the corners of the patient's eyelids would be stitched to keep them in place. Apart from being very frightening for everyone involved, this must be treated as a medical emergency because of the risk of damage to the optic nerve and, therefore, the baby's vision. All the equipment that might be needed in an emergency was kept by Lucy's bed, including saline and gauze.

Her trachy needed changing weekly and one day, in her mother's absence, I decided to do it. Having gathered all the necessary equipment together, I proceeded to take out the old tube and began to insert the new one. However, after struggling to insert it, I could not get the new tube in – I knew Lucy's airway was abnormal.

Starting to feel nervous, I decided to call for the anaesthetist because I didn't want to lose her airway. I instinctively pushed the emergency bell and two staff nurses came running.

'Get the anaesthetist. Quickly.' I instructed. One went off to phone the emergency number 5555 and the other staff nurse brought the rescuitation trolley into the cubicle.

The anaesthetist, a young man, had only just arrived to help put the trachy back in, when one of the nurses said, 'Her eye!' Alarmingly, one of Lucy's eyes had popped out of its socket on to her cheek, so I had two emergency situations to deal with at once.

'Put a saline soak over it,' I told her.

It happened so quickly, but I didn't panic – testament perhaps to how far I had come. A few years earlier and I would have been beside myself with anxiety.

'Just pop it back in,' I now instructed the staff nurse.

She took Lucy's eyeball and deftly, with a gloved hand and saline gauz, gently returned it to the socket. Meanwhile, I told the anaesthetist that I was having trouble replacing the child's trachy tube. He assessed the situation quickly and inserted the silver metal tracheal dilators to expand the windpipe, enabling him to put the tube in successfully.

Lucy started coughing until she was puce in the face, but I know I must have let out a sigh of relief – thank goodness she was okay. Gradually she settled down and appeared calmer.

The poor nurse who was 'specialling' the baby looked

very bewildered as she stood by watching the action unfold.

'I was paralysed to the spot when the eye came out,' she said. 'Thank God you were here when it happened, else I wouldn't have had a clue what to do.'

'That's why we are just outside,' I said. I tried to turn the situation into a teaching session so that she would feel more confident about looking after Lucy and we talked through everything that had happened, step by step.

Little Lucy stayed with us for about a week without any further dramas, and when she got over her viral infection she was transferred back to the neuro-surgical unit, where she was operated on to prevent other health problems arising, including brain damage. I lost track of how well she did but the prognosis was not good, which was very sad indeed.

I always felt well supported by the team of nurses we had on the ward. They were dedicated, efficient, and always willing to stay on to finish the work when we were particularly busy. I hope they, in turn, felt supported by me. I always made time for them if they wanted to discuss anything and I drummed into them the things that had been stressed to me: the child first and always; that they must always listen to the mother; and that they should always trust their instincts.

Of course, as ward sister, I had many difficult staffing issues to deal with as well as medical emergencies. I remember an occasion when Abelle came to me concerned about an agency nurse who had been looking after one of the patients. As we were short on the ward he had been brought in to 'special' a five-year-old boy, Tom, who had chickenpox and encephalitis, which is swelling of the brain tissue and a complication of this childhood disease.

The nurse was a young man and fairly nondescript; I had seen him around the ward but Abelle was more involved in Tom's care.

'He's getting too caught up in the emotional side of things,' she told me. 'I can't quite put my finger on it, but I'm worried. The way he is, well ... he keeps asking questions. It's just a bit odd.'

'What sort of things does he ask?'

'Well, each day he comes in and asks loads of things about Tom's parents, such as, are they happy in their marriage? Is Tom really loved by his father? It seems very inappropriate, given the situation at the moment.'

'And what do you make of his nursing?'

'He's appears to be good,' she said. 'He's calm, thorough and efficient. I've got no complaints there.'

'I'll talk to him,' I told her.

The following day I called the nurse into my office. At the time it just felt like an everyday staffing issue.

'Be careful not to get too involved,' I told him. 'We are here to help Tom get better in an acute situation in his little life. He'll go back to continue his family life however happy or unhappy it is.'

The young man nodded.

'It is not for us to interfere at this stage,' I continued. 'There are other people who look after the emotional side of things.'

He listened and acknowledged the truth of what I had said, then left the office.

The next day, the nurse did not come back to the ward and I presumed he had been sent elsewhere by the agency he worked for. There were huge numbers of staff on the wards, with rotas always changing, so I didn't think twice about it.

Many months later, I heard that this nurse had been suspended from another hospital for sexual abuse, pending investigation. One of the more senior staff brought it to my attention because she knew that we used the agency he worked for. I never heard the outcome, but suspect that if he was found guilty he would not have been allowed to work with children or vulnerable people again.

As this case also made its way into the newspaper, I decided to discuss the implications of the situation with Abelle.

'Look at this,' I said. She took the paper from me and started reading, looking more and more horrified the further she read.

'God, that is awful,' she said, gasping. 'I know I was with him most of the time, but could he have done anything to Tom?'

'I really don't know. I'm going to look into it.'

I was as surprised as she was about the situation.

'Would Tom have known? How dreadful,' she said.

'Try to put it out of your mind. I am mentioning it to everyone I can. There is a bigger investigation going on about this man.'

After talking with the medical and social care staff, we felt there was no evidence that Tom had been abused in any way. I never got to meet his mother, who must have been beside herself, but I did hear that she was pleased we had recorded what had been discussed and was satisfied that we had done everything we could.

When all was done and dusted, I praised Abelle for being so vigilant. It really hit home how valuable our sixth sense is.

# II

# Josie and Edward

In 1975, when I was told that half my ward would change to become a dermatology ward, I was far from happy. I had never nursed dermatology patients before and knew little about skin conditions and treatments. Furthermore, I had not been involved in these discussions and was upset that no one had consulted me about the changeover. There were to be other changes, too: any patient requiring ventilation would be sent to the intensive care unit and those with haematology or oncology conditions would be housed on the 3AB ward.

'I can't believe they didn't consult me,' I said to John over dinner, which we often cooked for each other. 'I won't have a clue what I'm doing.'

I tried to make the best of it and got my head down in the evenings to read up about syndromes and hereditary disorders of the skin and its immune function. The dermatology consultants, eager to stimulate my interest, were very good about explaining these to me. Enthusiasm spirals downwards; I knew I had to support the nurses on the ward so I tried to pretend that I welcomed the challenge.

The strong medicines and creams applied to the skin were strange to me at first, but I soon learnt their actions and started to become interested in what I was observing. It was like being back in my student days because I was acquiring masses of new information.

We saw many children with severe eczema, where the skin was very sore, and they had often developed other infections, some of which, such as herpes, could be life-threatening.

One of the most memorable patients in the early weeks was Josie, who came in with suspected epidermolysis bullosa, where the skin is so delicate that it blisters at the gentlest touch and 'falls off'. A lifelong genetic disorder, it only affects one in 50,000 people, whose skin lacks the protein that binds each layer together. Many of the children who suffer from this condition develop breathing problems, when blisters develop in the respiratory tract; the mouth can also be affected, making it difficult to eat, and such patients often lose their fingernails. Most children with this disease tended to be treated at GOSH at the time.

There are three major types of epidermolysis bullosa and on the ward we mostly saw children with the dystrophic type – the most serious. In this type, insufficient collagen is produced due to gene mutation, resulting in an almost non-existent connection between the layers of skin. The fingers and toes may fuse and curl over, and may need operating on, making it difficult for the patient to walk. The condition is extremely painful; even being picked up can be agony, not unlike suffering from a second-degree burn.

Josie was about six years old when I first met her and was deaf, but could lip-read very well. Small, with mousy hair and a gentle manner, she had just started school and was as bright as a button. She had been admitted to GOSH for assessment by her local hospital in Birmingham.

'I love school,' she announced when we first met. 'My teacher, Mrs Brucknell, says girls are nicer than boys. I think so too.'

'Well, you've come to the right place,' I told her. 'There is a teacher here who can do your reading with you. She likes girls too.'

'I want to be Jennifer Yellow-hat,' Josie continued, referring to the One, Two, Three and Away! books. 'She's better than Billy Blue-hat and Roger Red-hat.'

Josie's mother, Sarah, was a nurse and very patient with her. She stayed in the hospital accommodation at first, and came on to the ward every morning to show us how to change her daughter's dressings. In this case, we were the ones doing the learning and we would watch her carefully as she bandaged her child's arms, legs and torso.

Josie's skin was covered with open weeping wounds and many crimson scabs. They would take ages to heal, despite her mother's gentle care. She slept on smooth silk sheets to limit any friction, but even being touched would blister her delicate skin, which was like wet tissue paper. Sometimes her whole arm or leg would be without the top layer of skin.

'I call you my butterfly girl, don't I?' Sarah used to tell her daughter. She never voiced the sad fact that we all knew: Josie would never run around outside like her peers, play games like hide-and-seek, or have anything like an ordinary child's life. Her fun was restricted to gentle activities like playing ludo or snakes and ladders. She also loved reading and had a flat-toned voice, typical of someone who is deaf. She always wanted to play with the other children and couldn't understand why they needed to be in hospital. We were never allowed to answer her questions because of confidentiality, so she would bound over and ask the other children's mothers and they always told her.

Sarah would have to spend at least three hours a day cautiously changing her daughter's dressings; taking care not to dislodge the fragile skin as she took them off, giving her a bath in emulsifying ointment for at least half an hour, while also soaking some of the dressings in the oily water. She would dry her skin with a hair dryer, which made Josie cackle, apply any ointments, then put the new dressings on. It was a never-ending job and Josie would find it uncomfortable. Sarah would talk to her quietly all the time, sing silly songs or they would hum along to Abba to try and distract her. How Sarah managed to fit this time-consuming job around her own day job, and look after things at home, I would never know. She spoke warmly of her husband, a police-man, who was extremely supportive. Sarah explained that she was always the one who did Josie's care because she knew exactly how to do it. Sometimes, at weekends, Sarah would give Josie a day off from the painful pro-cedure, but her dressings would start to smell and this would make her very upset. Josie was in constant dis-comfort and sometimes pain.

'It breaks my heart to have to do it every day. She is very brave,' Sarah told us. 'It feels so strange sometimes holding her down. I don't know how much I'm hurting her, but I know it's a lot. I just want her to be happy.'

While Josie was with us, she had a skin biopsy to diagnose the type of skin condition she suffered from. She went to theatre to have a piece of skin removed for investigation and a couple of stitches were put in. It was quickly confirmed that it was dystrophica. Remarkably, the biopsy site healed well, which sur-prised everyone.

It was the middle of the summer when Sarah and Josie were with us. The days were so hot and sticky that my uniform was always soaked after a few hours of work. One day, when Sarah was heading home, I asked her if I could take Josie out for a walk in nearby Coram Fields. Nowadays, it would be necessary to get written consent to take a patient outside the hospital, but this wasn't the case then.

'Oh yes please, she'll love that,' Sarah replied. 'I know she'll be in good hands. It's not easy going out with her, as you can imagine. I'm always terrified she'll fall over or another child will run into her. Her friends often play around her and she hobbles after them, trying to join in. I do try to make life as normal as possible for her.'

Josie was very excited at the prospect of a walk. After my shift finished, we strolled back to my new flat in Lamb's Conduit Street, where I put her in front of the television while I had a bath. I couldn't wait to get my clothes off.

As I soaped away the day's sweat, Josie wandered into the bathroom, totally unembarrassed about my nakedness, as children are.

I was a bit shocked by this but tried to not let it show in my face.

'Sister, please can I have a drink?'

'Of course. There is some squash by the fridge and a glass there too. Be careful.'

These days it would be regarded as suspicious if a six-year-old said she had seen a nursing sister in the bath, but it wasn't then. Even so, I made a mental note to tell Sarah, so that if Josie said anything she would know what she was talking about. Then we set off on the short walk to the local park. Coram Fields, which is about a ten-minute walk away, is a unique place because adults are only allowed in if they are accompanied by a child. Neither are dogs or bicycles permitted, so I knew that Josie would be safe.

Josie loved it and she had an inquisitive mind, asking many questions about the flowers and people. 'Why are the children doing that?' 'What is that flower over there? Why is that little boy crying?' There was a never-ending list.

I grew very fond of Josie and her mother during their time at the hospital. Josie never moaned about her difficulties and seemed unaware of people seeing her differently. As she grew older, of course, she would become more conscious of this, but for now she was fun and a pleasure to care for. I felt privileged to play such an important part in her life, even though it was only for a short time.

It was at about this time that I became interested in a group called DEBRA, a charity working on behalf of people in the UK suffering from epidermolysis bullosa. I was invited to give a talk on it at a conference aimed at adults with the disease and parents whose children had it. At this event, I met many adults who had not been expected to live much longer than a few months. They said they found the condition extremely difficult to manage, especially as they often lost friends to the disorder. DEBRA worked in collaboration with GOSH in publishing leaflets for people who had the disease and also for those nursing children in hospital. The conference was the beginning of something much bigger. The charity funds research and there is now a full-time dermatology nurse/specialist, who is based at GOSH but covers the United Kingdom. There are now three other centres in the UK looking after children with the disorder and nurses who visit affected families to offer practical and emotional support. Over the years DEBRA has made important discoveries about the illness.

As many children on the ward were covered in thick emollients to soften their skin, it was very difficult to keep the place clean. The bed sheets were always stained with grease and our uniforms often got soiled, despite wearing gowns and disposable aprons and gloves when attending to the children. They would sometimes wrap their arms around our legs affectionately, trying to get our attention. It was imperative that we did not push them away, as the normal social reaction to people with skin disease; many people were under the mistaken impression that it was catching. We tried very hard to show affection by touching and cuddling the children, but it was difficult when they were covered in grease and you knew that a hug was imminent. I spent many hours cleaning myself up after shifts and was constantly washing my hands so that equipment didn't slip through my fingers.

Edward came to us for the first time when he was about ten years old and returned several times during the years I was on Cohen Ward. He had chronic eczema from head to toe and there wasn't a patch on his body that was not angry and scarlet. His skin was scaly, hard and dry in parts and he always had a number of open lesions. He had no eyebrows or eyelashes and you could see the rash on his scalp beneath his thin mop of bright blond hair. He scratched himself constantly, despite our painstaking bandaging of his hands and telling him that it would only make the problem worse. He was a quiet boy, very introverted and thoughtful, and unlike some children, he didn't seem able to relax, however long he stayed with us.

'Back again, are you, Edward?' I would say to him. 'You must really love the food here.' He would never laugh, just smile and quickly look away to avoid catching my eye.

He gave one-word answers to everything we asked him and resisted all our attempts to get him to open up. He spent most of his time on his own; his mother rarely visited him, so I didn't know much about his family situation.

Edward was admitted every few months or so when his eczema flared up and led to a secondary skin infection. As he was growing up and would soon be a teenager, I knew it was important for him to have physical contact so that he wasn't scarred mentally by his condition. The natural thing would be to recoil from some of these uglier skin diseases and we nurses made a conscious effort to touch him whenever it seemed appropriate. We always took time to give him hour-long daily baths and would then grease him all over with steroid creams to try and alleviate his suffering.

Regardless of his treatment, Edward's condition never really improved.

I heard later that he was to go into a home for young people after it was suggested that perhaps his home environment was not helping his illness. Taking a child away from his or her parents is always a huge decision; one I was fortunately never faced with. Due to the need for confidentiality, combined with the fact that we were always so busy, we never had a full picture of a child's life at home. In a typical case, GOSH would give an opinion as to the treatment required and the patient would be transferred to his local hospital. Occasionally the consultant would see the child in a follow-up outpatients' appointment and fill us in on any relevant information. It would have been lovely to have known what happened to all the children we had nursed, but that was seldom the case. Sometimes the parents and child would pay us a visit and it was always a happy, friendly occasion; they would tell us how they were getting on at school or what sort of job they were doing. Those who were coping less well with their difficulties, we rarely saw again.

Two years later, a young man walked into Cohen Ward. His head was held high and his eyes sparkled. More importantly, his skin was normal.

'Sister?'

I had to do a double take but the bright blond mop of hair gave him away. I couldn't believe my eyes.

'Edward! How are you?'

'Good, really good.'

'Your skin looks great.'

He held out his arms and hands and I couldn't believe it; his skin had healed so well and it was pale and smooth. He told me he had been for an outpatients' appointment, the first in more than six months.

'I want to go to university,' he said. 'I've just started my GCSEs. I want to be a doctor. I really like science. Last week we did some stuff with test tubes and Bunsen burners. It was so cool.'

He couldn't have been more different to the person who had once stayed with us. I think the dramatic turnaround must have been due to the change in his home environment. Edward was accompanied by a lovely round-faced lady in her fifties, who I thought must be his foster carer.

'So, any nice girls at school?' I teased him. 'Any girlfriends?'

'There might be some,' he said, getting all shy.

'Try lots,' said the lady he was with. 'There's at least one girl calling every night under the pretext of needing to know something for their homework.'

'I bet you're fighting the ladies off. And just wait until you get to university. A handsome young doctor-to-be, like you, they'll be queuing round the block for a date,' I told him.

Edward went as red as a beetroot and laughed.

His amazing recovery still remains one of the most miraculous changes I have ever seen in a child. I was so happy that Edward had found his feet.

By this time, I had moved out of my flat in Marble Arch as the lease had run out. The landlord had not warned us about it, so we managed to live there rent-free for another two months. My flatmates mostly had partners by then and were considering moving in with them. Since there was some urgency to find somewhere else, I moved into Spens House in Lamb's Conduit Street, where the rent was subsidised by the hospital. I was earning a little more by then but nothing to shout about, so the cheaper rent was very welcome. Spens House was known as 'The Virgins' Retreat' by the men at work because of the abundance of single nurses who lived there. Each flat consisted of a room that acted as both a bedroom and sitting room, with a separate kitchen and bathroom.

I liked it there and because it was just round the

corner from the hospital I was able to spend more time doing the Christmas show. We got to know some of the London Welsh Boys' Choir who practised round the corner and had magnificent voices. They asked me if I knew anywhere they could rehearse for a month, while their usual place was being redecorated, and I suggested the basement of the School of Nursing where we put on the Christmas show. One of the conditions was that they would appear in that year's show. The choir proved hugely popular with the audience and I managed to get them to perform two years running; they felt very honoured to be part of the hospital.

At that time, the slow bicycle race in the front drive of the hospital was another annual event and all the participants had to dress up. The rules were that you had to cycle as slowly as possible and keep your feet on the pedals. Bill Marshall held the record and there was much cheating. I never dared to enter as I couldn't allow him to beat me, but I always cheered extra loudly for his competitors. All the children and their parents would come out on to the balconies to watch.

We also had an annual Cohen barbecue for the nurses and their families in nearby Mecklenburgh Square where Bill Marshall had a flat and, therefore, the key to the wonderful gardens. The nurses were in charge of the food, the men the drink and lighting the barbecue. We all prayed for good weather and were usually lucky. John always came along with his colleagues from the hospital.

Although we normally saw each other in a group, John and I would also go to classical and folk music concerts or to the outdoor theatre in Regent's Park together, or the cinema if there was anything worth seeing.

I really had a soft spot for him and often invited

him over because I wanted to impress him with my cooking.

I remember one evening when I was having friends, including John, round for a roast chicken dinner. I was late home from work and in a rush as usual, but my old flatmate, Joan, said she would help me. She came home from work with me and we both set about making the meal.

We chatted in the kitchen while I prepared the chicken and potatoes and put them in the oven, and Joan chopped some vegetables and quickly tidied up. After popping into my room to get changed, I went back to the kitchen to baste the chicken, but when I opened the oven door it wasn't there.

'Joan, where is the chicken? Am I going mad? I just put it in!' I looked again – the oven was definitely empty.

'What? I have no idea. I've been doing the carrots!' she said.

I started to open the fridge door, then went through the kitchen cupboards, starting to question my own sanity. It was one of those days when I had been doing things so quickly that my brain wasn't quite keeping up.

After about ten minutes of this, Joan went out on to the balcony. The flat was on the fourth floor.

'Sue, come and have a look at this.'

'What?' I was starting to get annoyed and very flustered now. What would John think if he was presented with a meal of just potatoes and carrots?

I followed Joan on to the balcony and peered over.

There in the car park was my chicken, still cooking on my camping stove.

'Joan, that is NOT funny!' I shouted and stormed downstairs to retrieve it. By the time I returned, so had my sense of humour, and we both started laughing. When the guests turned up twenty minutes later, everything look spick and span.

Tucking in, John was particularly complimentary.

'This is delicious, Sue,' he said. 'Great chicken!'

Joan stifled a laugh, but I was secretly pleased that he liked it.

Along with the fun and socialising, work was sometimes very tough. One of the most distressing things I saw during my time on Cohen Ward was a baby with harlequin ichthyosis, another genetic abnormality. The disease is characterised by a profound thickening of the skin in huge diamond-shaped scales. Aaminah came to us as a newborn baby. She had a massive, horny shell of dense, plate-like scales and abnormalities of the eyes, ears, mouth, hands and feet. This disease limits movement and compromises the protective skin barrier, leaving the sufferer susceptible to metabolic abnormalities and infection. The term 'harlequin' derives from the patient's expression and the triangular and diamond-shaped pattern of plates of skin. The newborn's mouth is pulled wide open, mimicking a clown's smile. It was very distressing at first to see a child like this and we knew that the long-term prognosis was not good.

Aaminah's father was a well-to-do Asian businessman and he had been married to her mother for a couple of years. They had been trying for a baby since their wedding day and were understandably completely floored by her condition.

'Can you make her better? Will she be alright? Will she be able to lead a normal life?' They asked the same questions over and over again, demanding to see the doctors at every hour of every day.

'Why is her nose like that?' 'Why is she making those strange noises?' 'Will her feet always be so swollen?'

None of us had any answers for him. I could only reassure him that we were doing our best to help Aaminah.

The baby was nursed in a cubicle and the parents were insistent that the nurse stayed in there with them at all times.

'She *must* stay here. We might need something. Aaminah might need her,' her father demanded. 'I need answers to my questions.'

Reluctantly, I agreed to this until the baby had been assessed and her treatment had begun, but I knew we could not keep this up indefinitely. We just didn't have enough nurses to look after the rest of the children on the ward.

The baby's daily care took a long time, so the couple and the nurses were in the cubicle a good number of hours. We gave her baby baths, soaking her in an emollient solution then greasing the skin with soft white paraffin, and we covered her with bandages and dressings to keep the skin moist. Sometimes large pieces of thick skin would flake off, like large grey scabs. It was constantly upsetting for the parents, as they felt that they were somehow to blame and did not want any relatives to visit.

Despite the support they received, they would not accept that we could do nothing for Aaminah. I felt very sorry for them despite their constant demands.

'You must be able to do something, Sister. Please. This is not good enough,' Aaminah's father would say, many times a day.

As the days ticked by, the other nurses and I were constantly bombarded with demands and were told that we weren't doing enough to help Aaminah. While I gently suggested that the parents, too, could help, they never did. They just watched silently from the sidelines, eyes narrowed and dark, as if they were judging every move we made.

After two of my more junior nurses came to me in tears because the father had been argumentative and rude, I decided enough was enough.

I found them sitting in the cubicle with Aaminah as usual.

'Mr and Mrs Khan, please listen to me. We are doing our best. This is a very, very rare skin disease and many of us have never dealt with a baby with harlequin's before. We are doing everything within our power to help your daughter, but you must stop demanding an unreasonable amount of time and care. You could do more to help with Aaminah's care yourselves. We have shown you a number of times how to change her dressings.'

I would not have spoken to parents like that earlier in my career, but I had learnt by then that there are times when one has to be firm and direct if they are being unreasonable. I was well aware that distress and anxiety can affect behaviour, but I felt that, as an educated businessman, Aaminah's father should have been more understanding.

They sat in silence, stony-faced.

'Think about what I have said,' I concluded and left the cubicle. I was pleased that I had finally plucked up the courage to tackle the situation head-on, and tried to busy myself with other things.

A couple of hours later, when I hoped they had had enough time to think about it, I went to find them and explained that I hadn't meant to be so blunt, but that it had needed to be said to clear the air.

'My nurses are upset. They really are trying to help Aaminah, and so am I. We are all on your side.'

'Maybe there is more we can do to help,' they conceded.

After that, our relationship was cordial at best, but they were less demanding and started doing a little more to help make Aaminah's life easier.

I knew that Aaminah would have this skin disorder for life and that the attitude of parents and child would be paramount in how they would all cope with her abnormality. Sadly, the prognosis was not good in those days. I lost touch with the family, so can only imagine that little Aaminah would have been kept at home and not been allowed to mix with other children, or with adults, or she might have died in early childhood. Aaminah's grandmother might have helped with her care, but the child would probably have been left in her cot, rocking backwards and forwards in distress. I very much hoped that this was not allowed to happen, but if she lived, Aaminah would have needed long-term, local social care.

During my time on Cohen Ward, the speciality of immunology, the study of the immune system, was being developed. Many of the doctors worked in research, as well as doing their day jobs, and one of the most notable was a South African, Dr Roland Levinsky. He worked with the consultant immunologist Professor Soothill, and was always moaning that no beds were allocated to patients with immuno-deficiency, where the immune system is absent or defective. The immune system is made up of a network of cells, tissues and antibodies that work together to protect the body from invading foreign substances such as bacteria or viruses.

Dr Bill Marshall had done much work in developing a vaccination against rubella, also known as German measles, now given in combination with measles and mumps (MMR) to all children between twelve and eighteen months old. He had also made an important contribution to the research on congenital rubella syndrome, which can occur in the foetus of a pregnant woman if she has contracted rubella during her first trimester. Dr Marshall was interested in the work of Dr Levinsky and offered to lend him a bed on Cohen Ward.

It was Roland Levinsky who performed the first bone marrow transplant at GOSH in 1979 and I remember the occasion well. His continuing research into gene therapy has provided the basis for much of the successful work today in gene transplantation.

A lot of planning had to go into this procedure before it could be undertaken. We had to search for a 'clean air' system because the child would have no immunity in the early stages of transplant and would be very susceptible to infection. The environment is full of bacteria, fungi and sometimes viruses transmitted by other people. Our immune systems do battle with these daily and effectively, but children with immunological deficiency disorders are prone to infection after losing their mothers' protective antibodies about four to six months after birth.

They are just as vulnerable when they undergo a bone marrow transplant, especially to fungal infections, which are difficult to treat and can be fatal. Fungi are common in the environment and until the immune system is functioning normally, the child might be nursed in a 'clean air system' where all the air is filtered and prevents these organisms invading the child's respiratory system.

We eventually found a company which manufactured a plastic tent-like apparatus called a 'Bubble'. It had a HEPA filter in the top (which filters out 99.9 per cent of germs) and was just large enough to hold a cot. The air inside had to be under positive pressure to enable the amount of oxygen to remain the same as in normal air and to prevent dust and other organisms from entering the tent. Nowadays, 'clean air' systems are built into the fabric of hospitals, but it was a completely new concept back in the 1970s – almost experimental. We measured the cubicle carefully and found that the Bubble would just fit, giving us access to the handwash sink inside.

The first child to have a bone marrow transplant had been normal at birth and had thrived in the first three weeks of life. He had then developed a chest infection, followed by severe thrush infections and, at seven weeks, a further upper respiratory chest infection with a red rash on his skin. When, at fifteen weeks, he developed septicaemia, he was transferred to GOSH for diagnosis and found to have congenital immune-deficiency. To save his life he needed a bone marrow transplant from a suitable donor. Three weeks later, when he and his three-year-old brother were found to be compatible, he was given the transplant.

Almost a year after the first transplant, a six-year-old girl called Fiona came in for one too. She was suffering from a rare blood disorder, aplastic anaemia, meaning that she failed to produce new blood cells. She had been diagnosed a few months earlier, when admitted with pale skin, dizziness and weakness, and her parents had been told that without a transplant she might not live more than six months. So started a desperate race to find a match.

Fiona's mother, Annie, told me that both she and her husband were high-powered City workers and they employed a nanny at their Hampstead home.

'Our whole world just collapsed,' she said. 'Nothing seemed to matter any more. The holidays, money, nothing. I gave up my job, laid off the nanny and prayed.'

Tests were carried out on the family. Neither she nor her husband was a match; nor was Fiona's twin brother, Jack. But her eight-year-old sister, Suzy, was.

'Suzy had been desperate to help Fiona,' she said. 'I got the call just before I picked her up from school and when I told her she started crying, then went back to tell her teacher she was going to save her little sister.'

Annie's eyes started welling up as she told me their story.

'Suzy is only eight and I hate the thought of putting her through a painful operation but we don't have any choice. Fiona is getting sicker by the day.'

To enter the cubicle, I and the other nurses had to wear a gown, mask and hair cover and then wash our hands. We would unzip the tent inside the cubicle to enter and the zip would be done up while we were in there. The noisy buzz of the air filter was quite loud but Annie and Fiona soon got used to it.

'It reminds me of a buzzy bee,' Fiona told me.

We had to plan ahead carefully as it was a major exercise if we forgot anything. A baby alarm allowed us to communicate with Annie inside the Bubble and she with us. Unfortunately this only worked well if we spoke clearly as it was prone to crackling, perhaps due to interference as we were sometimes close by.

'Testing, testing, one, two, three,' she would say.

'Please can we have some orange juice in here? Madam says she is thirsty.'

Inside the cubicle we showed Annie how to clean the walls of the tent, the bed, locker and floor.

'Gosh, I'm not used to getting my hands dirty,' she said with a laugh. When all the areas were dry she would leave the mop and bucket outside the tent. The nurse would clean the cubicle ledges, sink and floor, and finally the mop and bucket would be cleaned outside, ready for the next session.

Annie was understandably eager to be completely vigilant, as any germs could spell disaster for her daughter. She had to make sure she was well each day and not showing signs of a sore throat, cold or tummy upset, and the same applied to the nursing staff as any infection could be fatal. Fiona was first admitted to GOSH during the winter months, when coughs and colds were unavoidable, but we managed to adjust the rota to cope with this. Along with the staff, only Annie and her husband were allowed into the cubicle. Suzy and Jack would come and talk to Fiona through the intercom, which was very sweet to hear.

'Can you hear me, FiFi?' Jack said one day. 'Daddy and I took Boris for a walk last night.'

'I miss Boris,' Fiona replied.

'Boris misses you too. He sends you a lick.' He then made a slurping noise and they both started giggling.

Fiona's immune system had to be weakened in preparation for the transplant. This involved destroying the diseased cells in order to stimulate the bone marrow to make its own good new cells. This would also help to prevent her body from rejecting the new bone marrow. This made Fiona feel sick and miserable, but

Annie would try and take her mind off it by reading to her.

Fiona's sister Suzy was admitted on another ward and I went to the theatre to watch the operation to gather her bone marrow. It was exciting to be involved in something that was so revolutionary and I felt privileged to be part of a team that enabled procedures like these to happen.

Under a general anaesthetic, a bone-marrow needle was inserted into Suzy's hip bone and the bone marrow aspirated into a blood-giving bag. The needle was moved around under the skin and redirected into the bone in order to collect as much marrow as possible. It looked painful because it was so invasive.

Suzy then recovered on the ward. She was groggy and sore, with some bruising, and was given painkillers for twenty-four hours after the procedure. But she didn't complain and kept asking, 'Will Fiona be better now?'

The blood bag containing the bone marrow was then taken into the Bubble, connected to a transfusion set and infused into Fiona. Observations were taken every fifteen to thirty minutes and it took some three to four hours.

'I just want to know if it has worked,' Annie said anxiously as we carried out the procedure. It would be several weeks before we could begin to answer that question.

Suzy only stayed in the hospital for one night, and when she had recovered, she would come and wave through the Bubble at her little sister.

'When can I hug my sister?' she would ask me. 'I love her. I want to cuddle her. Is she going to be alright?'

'I really hope she will be, sweetheart. We are doing

everything we can to help her and hopefully she will be better again soon.'

'I want Mum to come home,' she added. 'Daddy's cooking is rubbish!'

Regular blood tests were taken to monitor Fiona's blood count and see if the bone marrow was recovering. Fiona stayed in the Bubble for about eight weeks until her white cells had been restored to normal. Fiona's parents fine-tuned a visiting routine: Annie would appear on the ward after dropping Jack and Suzy off at school and their father would relieve her after work, rushing down the corridor clutching his briefcase.

Annie came to trust us implicitly with Fiona's care and after a while she felt sufficiently confident to go home at night – it was only a twenty five-minute journey on the tube from Holborn to Hampstead. About six weeks after the transplant Annie developed a cold, so we advised her to stay at home until it was better; as well as the obvious risk to Fiona, we couldn't risk the staff catching it.

When she was well again, and if we were not too busy, Annie would come into my office for a chat.

'We're going out for a meal tonight,' she told me towards the end of Fiona's treatment. 'We're even letting the kids decide where we go, so we may end up at McDonald's. I've been feeling so low and we thought it might cheer us all up. Suzy and Jack miss Fiona terribly. They used to argue all the time but now they can't wait for her to come home.'

Later that evening, she called with the name of the restaurant – luckily for Annie it wasn't McDonalds – and I reassured her that we would contact her if anything changed. She knew she could call us any time, day or night.

When the results of the blood test came through indicating that Fiona's bone marrow had started to recover, we entered the ward with big smiles and gave a thumbs-up sign through the wall of the Bubble. Annie let out a whoop of joy into the intercom.

We were already planning to take Fiona out of the Bubble and keep her in one of the cubicles before she returned to the ward.

'If her blood count stays as good as this on Wednesday, she can come out,' I told Annie, much to her delight. I had been badgering the doctors to reach a decision.

'Okay. I'm not going to tell Jack and Suzy, because if it doesn't happen there will be rivers of tears. I'm just going to let them think they are coming in to wave at Fiona as normal!'

We all held our breath as we waited for Fiona's latest blood test results and when good news came back, and it was agreed with the doctors that she could come out, I found myself punching the air. Annie was jumping up and down inside the Bubble, with Fiona in her arms.

After the initial delight had worn off, I knew that Fiona's parents would be concerned that she might pick up something from the other children, such as a viral infection. We warned them that this could happen, but reassured them that Fiona's immune system should now be strong enough to fight it.

The reunion with her siblings was a scene I will remember for ever. Jack and Suzy came in with their father after school, each holding a hand and wearing their smart school uniforms. As they turned into the ward, of course they expected to see Fiona in the Bubble and at first looked very confused. Instead, the sight that greeted them was Fiona sitting up in bed playing with a toy, while Annie sat next to her, smiling manically.

'FiFi,' Jack said, launching himself across the room at his twin, in a way that only little boys can, his school cap falling off in the process.

Suzy stood motionless, her eyes wide with disbelief, then started to cry. There was a moment when no one knew what to say.

'Come here, silly,' Annie said, beckoning her over, 'I haven't had a chance to say thank you.'

Suzy went over and gave her mother a huge hug.

By this point, both parents and all the nurses were in floods of tears. It was so lovely to see a family reunited after such a long time apart. And it was a wonderful triumph for the hospital: another little life had been saved.

# 12

# Sharing Our Knowledge

I n 1980, after eight years of being a ward sister, the Chief Nursing Officer Betty Barchard told me about a six-month secondment in Jordan, teaching nursing care at the university hospital in Amman. Would I be interested?

I had previously felt envious of staff who had been seconded to the Mulago Children's Hospital in Kampala, Uganda. An exchange had run from 1959 until 1971, when the dictator Idi Amin came to power and relations broke down. The staff who had been part of it had had such interesting stories to tell about their time away that I felt they had experienced something special. They had also seen many illnesses that were common in Uganda such as polio, malnutrition and tetanus. Betty assured me that my job on Cohen Ward would still be open to come back to, so I didn't need to think twice about accepting. It was agreed that Abelle would take over running the ward and she was very excited when I told her about her new role. I knew the team would support her and that she wouldn't let me down.

When I mentioned the possibility to my mum, she encouraged me to go, even though she was anxious for me because Amman was so far from home.

'Sue, you must go,' John told me. 'It will be a great challenge. I'll write.'

I knew I would miss him and hoped he would be there

for me when I got back; I secretly thought he would, but there was still an element of doubt. He later admitted that he had missed me, but that was as much as he would say.

Preparing to leave, I packed and unpacked my bags several times, as there was so much to think of and so much to take. I was going in January, when it would be cold in Amman, and staying until the summer, when it would be very hot and dry. More importantly, I couldn't afford for my bags to be overweight.

I was unable to sleep on the overnight flight because I was both excited and anxious as to what I would find. As we left the departures area at Queen Alia International Airport, I was hit by a cacophony of noise; all the men appeared to be yelling at each other, as if they were spoiling for a punch-up. I soon realised that it was their natural way of talking – loudly, animatedly and without pausing. They waved their arms wildly, spoke quickly and kissed one another on both cheeks. I couldn't understand a word they said, nor could I interpret their body language. The men reminded me of pelicans fluffing their feathers, and appeared to dominate the women and children, who walked a few paces behind them, subservient and subdued.

When I stepped outside the airport, the smell hit me: a combination of oil, burnt kerosene from the aircraft and what can only be described as camel dung. A thin layer of powder hung as if suspended in the air.

The women were dressed in rainbow-coloured robes down to their ankles, with traditional Palestinian embroidery in geometric shapes down the front, which I later discovered symbolised good health, hope, prosperity and protection. They also wore hijabs – headscarves draped around their faces in line with their Muslim faith. The men were clothed in less flamboyant robes, with headscarves wound tightly into turbans around their heads, like colourful crowns.

As I peered out of the car window, which was smeared with dirt, muddy cars swerved around each other on the roads, beeping with abandon. I held on tightly to the door handle, as we zigzagged through the crowded streets towards our destination. There had been unseasonal rainfall and the puddles appeared to sit like pools of oil on the dry earth. The buildings looked dilapidated and were mostly made of concrete. There was much building work going on, from which it was evident that the whole area was in the process of development.

When I arrived at my new home, there was a message to say that the hospital matron, Cathy, would be coming to welcome me and give me lunch. Everything seemed so strange and foreign. The ground floor flat which I was to occupy, had a sitting room with a balcony, overlooking another chalky-coloured building, and one bedroom. There was a small kitchen with a portable gas stove, on which I would presumably have to cook my meals, and a simple bathroom. The floors were of white marble, to keep the flat cool.

I suddenly felt homesick, an uncomfortable feeling which made my stomach churn and my head pound. I thought about John and wondered what he was doing and if he might be wondering whether I had arrived safely. I also felt grubby with sweat and grime after all the hours of travelling, so peeled off my layers of clothes and ran the bath – thankfully there was plenty of hot water. As I lay back enjoying the feeling of the water on my skin, I wondered whether I would last the six months.

Surely it won't be that bad? I tried to think positively but my temples continued to throb. I thought of home and the familiarity of my day-to-day life at the hospital. Most of all I knew I would miss my friends, family and John. I was already looking forward to the letters they had promised to write, filling me in on the latest news and gossip.

Afterwards I lay back on my new bed and closed my eyes. I slept surprisingly well and woke only just in time for lunch with Matron.

There was a knock at the door and there stood a Jordanian man, the driver, who explained that he had come to take me to the hospital to meet Matron Cathy. I knew that I should be subservient in my behaviour, having been told that looking a man in the eye was a 'come on'. I tried to lower my eyes and bat my eyelashes but it felt slightly ridiculous. I didn't know whether to sit in the front seat of the car next to the driver or in the back seat, so I chose the latter. He spoke a little English and appeared friendly, but I wasn't taking any chances. When we arrived, the hospital was busy but looked uncared for inside, with a really old-fashioned feel to it. It smelt strongly of a different type of disinfectant from the one I was used to. But sure enough, after a few days I ceased notice the smell.

I was taken to the matron's office and told to wait outside, she would be with me very shortly. After about five minutes Cathy appeared. She was British and in her early forties, with wavy fair hair drawn up into a bun.

'Susan, so good to meet you. I'm so sorry I didn't come and fetch you myself,' she said. 'I've been caught up with a problem which I was obviously expected to sort out myself. I'm sure you know the sort of thing.'

I laughed. She had put me completely at ease.

'I'm so pleased you're here,' she continued. 'We could certainly do with some help.'

She gave me four sets of white trouser suits for my uniform and quickly started gathering her own things together.

'Right, let's go back to my flat. We'll have some lunch and I can tell you what things are like here.'

The day started early, at around 6.30 a.m. This was by far the coolest time, she explained, and it was almost a pleasure to be up and about before the searing heat kicked in. My shift would be from 7 a.m. until 2 p.m., with Fridays off, and because I was to work Saturdays and Sundays. I would have no two-day weekends. However, I liked Cathy and decided that my secondment was going to be fine. She told me a bit about the hospital, where she had been matron for two years, explaining that it was very different from those in the UK and nursing standards were quite low. The nurses were mostly Indian and Pakistani, with a few Jordanian nurses in higher positions. She warned me that I might be shocked by the attitude of the doctors towards the nurses. Even though it is now a big, thriving university hospital, it still had a long way to go then.

I was up early the next morning, ready for the car that would take me to the hospital. I went first to Cathy's office and she took me straight to the paediatric ward where she put me in the hands of the senior nurse, Sana, a short Jordanian woman with thick, wiry hair. Sana took me into her office, where we had coffee while she told me about the patients – fortunately she spoke good English. I explained that I was here to share my nursing knowledge and to help her run a good ward. Then she showed me around and introduced me to the doctors who appeared very friendly.

I spent the first few weeks on the paediatric ward getting to know the system and absorbing the cultural differences. It was not unusual for parents, who were mostly Muslim, to roll out their mats anywhere on the ward during prayer time. They would kneel down and start chanting wherever they could find some space, even in the treatment and resuscitation rooms. If these rooms were needed urgently, then the nurses or doctors would yell at the parents to move out of the way quickly. I felt this was disrespectful and suggested that visitors should simply be asked not to use them. That would have made no difference, I was told.

Several incidents occurred within the first weeks which shocked me to the core. These were mainly concerned with the doctors' behaviour. On one morning round, the senior consultant appeared with a lighted pipe in one hand and puffed away on his exotic tobacco as he went from patient to patient. Some doctors, while taking blood samples, would have a cigarette in one hand and a needle in the other. When they needed both hands, they would transfer the cigarette to their mouths and suck on it, dropping ash at their feet. During coffee time, I would bring these issues up while the doctors were present, but they just shrugged their shoulders as if unaware that smoking when attending to patients was wrong or even dangerous. If the consultants did it, why shouldn't they? I had to remind myself that in their eyes I was only a woman, and also only a nurse. Nurses in Jordan had a low social standing and were mostly expected to stay at home.

I also noticed that personal space was different here. Many of the assistant nurses would invade my space and give me a kiss on the cheek, leaving a bright red lipstick outline. I knew it was a sign of affection, but that was certainly not the way I was used to greeting my own staff. However, I didn't say anything because it was more important to make sure that we got on well.

Some of the children had pressure sores, especially those with hydrocephalus, where their heads were very large due to excessive fluid on the brain. These children's ears would often be eaten away with the pressure, which would not have happened if they had been turned frequently. Many children were admitted with empyema – pus in the cavity around the lungs – and required a chest drain because their lung had collapsed. To my horror, the nurses would disconnect the tubing from the underwater seal and shake the pus down the tube without clamping the chest drain. The drain is situated between the lung and the lining of the lung, called the pleural space, and if air gets in then the lung collapses, causing acute respiratory distress. To avoid this, the drain from the chest must be clamped before disconnection and failing to do so was a sure way of collapsing the lung further, but when I questioned it, I was told that the pus was so thick that it didn't matter. The Jordanian nurses responded so nonchalantly to my questions that I almost started to question my own judgement and learning.

I remember another incident well. As soon as I came on duty I always went straight to the baby bay. On this occasion, I noticed a baby in an incubator who looked very sick, with blue lips. He should have been on a ventilator, except that I found it was switched off.

'Why is this ventilator switched off?' I asked the nurse.

She gasped and ran to switch it back on.

'I switched it off while I listened to the baby's heart-beat,' she told me.

By this time I was sure the baby was dead. I had no idea how long the ventilator had been off, but it must have been a while. I called Sana over to deal with the situation and told her in straight language what I had seen. I was appalled and felt as if I might be sick.

On ward rounds I noticed that the doctors often fiddled with the electric switches; turning them on and off, as if they had nervous tics. They seemed completely oblivious to that fact that these were often connected to some piece of apparatus.

'Why do you keep switching the ventilators off?' I asked when I noticed one of the doctors reach for one of the switches yet again.

'So I can hear the heartbeat,' he told me.

Nonsense, I thought. It is dangerous to do that. Very dangerous.

Later I was saddened to hear that the baby whose ventilator had been disconnected had died. When I asked Sana how she had dealt with the nurse whose negligence had caused the baby's death, she just shrugged her shoulders.

'The nurse was tired,' she said. 'It is just one of those things that happens.'

I had to restrain myself from shaking her by her narrow shoulders. I realised there was a lot of teaching to do in the short time I was here and felt at a complete loss as to where to begin. It was as if I was just one small person flailing around in a rudderless boat on an ocean of problems. There did not seem to be any policies or guidance to draw on, either. In the end, I decided that the most important thing was to be a good role model and set an example as to what was acceptable practice.

I had many discussions with Cathy, who said that the whole hospital had problems. Often I felt exasperated by the situation, but she encouraged me keep up the good work. While we couldn't expect things to improve overnight, she was sure it was making a difference. I felt sorry for her as well. The doctors dominated the hospital and did not appear to want to change these unsafe practices – or perhaps, despite their arrogance, they did not know how to. The nurses were, as always, just seen as having supporting roles.

On another occasion, I was showing a mother and some nurses how to bath her baby, someone was interpreting for me, as the mother was a Bedouin and lived in the desert. She was wearing a long blue robe and was tiny and petite, almost like a child herself. She listened intently while the bathwater was running and was smiling as if she agreed, so I gently lifted the baby over the bath and went to put him into the water. In a flash, the mother started shouting hysterically in Arabic and snatched the baby from me, with such force that I was stunned. She was obviously frightened and upset, but I no idea why she had behaved in the way she did. The nurse who was interpreting couldn't understand her behaviour either, but although she went to talk to the mother, she didn't think to come back and tell me what had happened. I became engrossed in work again and the incident slid to the back of my mind.

A little while later, the mother reappeared and grabbed my arm. She seemed happier now, but was also very forceful. She pulled me into the bathroom off the side of the ward and, before I realised what was about to happen, had pushed me under the shower and switched it on. The water cascaded over my uniform and into my eyes. I was drenched from head to toe. At last, I began to realise what she had thought I was about to do to her baby. She was all wide smiles by now and I realised I had gained her trust.

Later, the interpreter told me why she had behaved in such a strange manner.

'She thought you wanted to drown her baby,' he said.

My head spun, but it made total sense.

'These women, they never waste water bathing. It is only used for cooking and drinking. Water is very precious in the desert. Bathing is not common. They don't understand it.'

Another memory that will stay with me forever was the admission of a young boy, who must have been about nine, with what looked like a deep knife cut in his leg. It was right down to the bone and oozing blood. However, he wasn't crying or showing any outward signs of distress. When I asked the consultant dermatologist what had happened, he replied, 'The child has split-skin syndrome.' I had never heard of this, even after my many years of dealing with skin conditions on Cohen Ward. He caught the confused look on my face, but appeared reluctant to say more. My fellow nurses seemed to have heard of it, but were unable to explain the cause.

When I had a moment, I consulted the dermatologist again because this child preyed on my mind.

'What is this split-skin syndrome?' I asked. 'I have never seen it, or heard of it before.'

'The parents told me the spirits did it in their home,' he replied. 'Their other children have been affected with this in the past. The only one who has never been touched by these spirits is Aseel who works at the hospital. He does not live at home.'

Spiritualism was very common in Jordan, but Western medicine was very new to the population, so we had a doubly difficult job on our hands. The people believed that any illness was caused by upsetting the spirits. It was important, for the child's sake, not to disbelieve the parents' explanation, as they would have taken their child away from the hospital. I now understood why the consultant's earlier explanation had been so guarded. This was a kind of 'Wassem', an increasingly outdated tradition, and one of the worst I had seen. The parents had branded his skin with a red-hot poker, causing burns, believing it would get rid of the 'evil spirits'. However, these traditions were very rare, and don't occur today.

Such treatment of children was inexplicable in Western eyes, but we needed to respect the sensitivity of the local beliefs, and accept the fact that we were strangers, and visitors to their world. They certainly had a long journey ahead of them, but we hoped that our small contribution would help them forward a few steps.

After I had been at the university hospital for a few months, another extremely harrowing incident occurred, when a baby boy was rushed into the resuscitation room after collapsing. I am not sure what caused it, but as always in these cases there were many doctors and nurses rushing around. The mother, a Jordanian, was in the room and watching closely as intravenous drips were inserted into the baby's arm and the doctors attempted to resuscitate him. Despite persistent efforts to revive the child, he died.

When the doctor walked over to tell the mother that

they could do no more, she let out a haunting cry, like that of an animal, and fell weeping and screaming to her knees.

Sana was present and, to my horror, started shouting at the mother in Arabic, like an irate fishwife.

'Look how our people react. They are so stupid,' she said to me, as if she was ashamed of the woman's behaviour.

She then went over to the wailing mother and kicked her in the side of her ribs.

'Get up,' Sana yelled.

I literally couldn't believe what I was seeing. It was as if I was in the middle of some sort of horrible nightmare. The blood rushed around my head, making me dizzy with emotion and anger.

'Don't do that!' I shouted at Sana. 'Her baby has just died! Have some compassion.' I rushed to the mother's side and put my arm around her and stroked her back.

Sana stormed out of the room, letting the door swing shut behind her. She was clearly very angry with me.

I helped the mother into a chair and let her hold the dead baby, who by now was wrapped in a blanket and free of all equipment. She couldn't speak any English, but I sat with her while she sobbed quietly, slowly calming down as she rocked the baby in her arms. I was very upset by the situation and at a loss to understand why Sana seemed so unsympathetic.

Eventually, the doctor came in with the father and took the mother and dead child away. I went to look for Sana but could not find her anywhere. Ten minutes later, a phone message was given to me to go and see Matron.

I went down to Cathy's office and she seemed to know

what had happened. I recounted the event as unemotionally as I could manage, and she said she thought it would be advisable for me to work in the nursing office for a few days. I don't know what Sana had told her but I felt bad about the situation, as though I had failed somehow.

The next day Sana was off duty so I did not see her for while. I realised there had been a clash of culture between us; she would have seen the mother as having no dignity, and I wanted to apologise. I still felt she should not have treated the mother in the way she did, but knew that for the sake of our working relationship we should have a discussion about it. When I did see her again, she was very cool, but appeared to have accepted my apology. I'm not sure our relationship would have survived if I had stayed on the ward. In the end, Cathy decided to keep me in the office to help her with her work, so I never never had to put it to the test again.

While assisting Cathy, I learnt about the recruiting process. Hundreds of applications rolled in from Indian and Pakistani nurses. I'm sure many of these were not written by the nurses themselves but by someone in their family. It was another world to learn about. I also used to check the ward duty rotas, help with writing up policies, file medical charts and attend meetings about potential changes. It doesn't sound much but the flow of work was never-ending. There were always people coming in with complaints which had to be investigated.

My social life in Jordan was mostly with Cathy and the British friends she had made. There were very few expats in our field at that time, so she had teamed up with people who held different jobs. She happily invited me to participate in whatever they were doing. From about March onwards, I sweated constantly and needed two or three showers a day to stay cool. It was very dusty and the sand from the desert got everywhere, from the inside of my suitcase to the sheets on my bed. Some days after being outside, I seemed to be coated in a fine dusting of it. The desert landscape was stunning, with colours that ranged from soft pink to immaculate white, with rocky outcrops. We went on picnics in the desert when it was so hot that the butter would melt before the sandwiches from the cool box reached our mouths and we visited many ancient sites, such as amphitheatres, and some amazing Byzantine forts. There was so much history in Jordan.

Over Easter we went to visit Jerusalem; it took about six hours to cross the border as there were so many restrictions. We met up with some of Cathy's friends on arrival and stayed with them for four days, visiting places of interest. Many of the attractions were closed as it was Passover, but we all had a good time in each other's company.

I was beginning to settle down, but I was still homesick at times and loved having letters from my friends. For once, I was fairly prompt in replying, making time to tell them about what I was seeing and doing, and how I felt. John's letters were short, sweet and badly punctuated.

'Dear Sue,' he would write. 'I hope you are well I played squash yesterday and won! Back to the grindstone today. John X'

To be honest, I was amazed that he wrote at all. Looking back now, I realise he must have been fond of me, he just couldn't express it.

My girlfriends' letters were much more enlightening and helped to keep me in touch with what was going on at home and in the hospital. They also told me much more about John than he did himself and I found them very comforting in my occasional lonely moments. During my last couple of months in Jordan, I read in the English newspapers about an outbreak of salmonella at GOSH. The press coverage made me wish I was there to help them deal with it.

My regular driver was a lovely man and during my last week in Amman he invited Cathy and me for a meal at his home one evening. It was a stark concrete building, consisting of a couple of small rooms for himself, his wife and three children. They all slept in one room and the other was their living area. We were beckoned to sit down on mats laid out on the floor. I knew that I must not show the bottoms of my feet because it was considered discourteous, so I tucked them under my long skirt and sat down as elegantly as I could manage.

One of the driver's sons was ushered in to sit with us; he was about ten years old and smiled politely. It seemed wrong that the driver's wife and the other children were outside preparing the meal, but it would have been inappropriate for them to join us. We were talking and laughing away, drinking cups of tea, and then his son fetched a bowl of warm water and a bar of Lux toilet soap so that we could wash our hands. The father and son then carried in a huge tray of goat's meat, rice and spices and we were told to start eating. I was enjoying myself so much that, being left-handed, I put my left hand into the rice, rolled some into a ball and popped it in my mouth. My tastebuds were on fire; it was delicious.

There was an awkward hush and Cathy whispered,

'Use your other hand!' I had forgotten how rude it was to use your left hand to eat with; this is because the left hand is used for dirty tasks such as wiping your bottom. I looked up sheepishly and apologised. The father smiled. I knew I had been forgiven and continued eating with my right hand.

Cathy then muttered to me under her breath, 'Don't eat too much as this is their meal for the next few days.'

We were honoured guests and the family had slaughtered a goat from their herd to mark the occasion. At the time, I had not realised how much they had sacrificed to entertain us like this; I knew my driver was not paid very much and he had his whole family to support. He regaled us with stories about his children; he was particularly proud of his eldest son, who was doing well at school. We had a lovely time and were very grateful to have experienced true Jordanian hospitality.

I had made many friends during my time in Jordan and was sorry and yet also glad to leave when the time came. I must confess to having shed a tear or two on the way to the airport that I had arrived at seemingly such a short time ago. I did not feel I had made a great difference, as the problems at the university hospital went far beyond the paediatric department. However, I felt I had learnt a lot about life and also about myself – certainly to be more patient and to respect the Jordanian way of life and culture. Many years later I was invited back to the hospital to give a talk, and could not believe the change. A thriving university hospital with up-to-date equipment and some much improved standards of care. As they say, 'from little acorns grow big trees'. I felt good that I had played a very small part.

As the plane climbed through the heat haze and

headed out across the Jordanian desert, I thought of those Bedouin people below, with their precious water and ancient spiritual beliefs, slowly finding their way into the modern world. I must have dozed off during the long flight dreaming of the desert.

I awoke with a start somewhere over Kent and looked down on to green fields as far as the eye could see, in the intermittent drizzle. I had not realised quite how much I had missed green fields and rain. I was glad to be back.

# 13

# The War on Infection

When I returned to GOSH, I hurried back to Cohen Ward. Abelle had managed the ward very well in my absence and it was good to catch up with everyone, especially John, who took me out for dinner and even bought me a bunch of flowers. He was very interested in my experiences and asked question after question about what I had seen and done while I was away.

He also filled me in on the hospital news. I learnt that the salmonella outbreak had caused many problems and involved a number of wards, and had been much in the news at the time. Tragically, one of the kitchen porters had committed suicide by throwing himself down a stairwell. He had become very depressed at the time, believing he had contributed to the problem because salmonella is found in raw and undercooked food. Of course, he was not to blame and the whole hospital was in shock: everyone felt guilty about what had happened. It was decided to put a strong, white net covering around the stairwell, because if this could happen to an adult, children could also have been at risk. At the time of the outbreak, the cause was unknown, although there was a suggestion that some of the samples that tested positive might have been contaminated in the lab. The evidence was no longer available to permit the kind of investigation that would be undertaken today, but the incident did lead to a number of changes for the better.

Among these was the hospital's decision to advertise for an infection control nurse. I felt I knew a good deal about infection and infectious diseases after working on Cohen Ward, and decided it was time to rise to a new challenge.

I was the only applicant so, of course, I got the job! Little did I know then quite how big this job would turn out to be.

Abelle got the job as sister on Cohen Ward. I was really delighted for her and confident that she would take up the baton and make a success of it. I felt ready for my next challenge and was promoted to nursing officer for the new job. My uniform was a turquoise short-sleeved dress with a white frilly hat.

Although I thought I knew all about infections, when I started the job, the terminology was like a new language; a scientific, microbiological, laboratory language. I was familiar with the more common bacteria, viruses, fungi and parasites which infect people, but there were many others I hadn't heard of. The same applied to the names of the micro-organisms – they all had at least two Latin names and sub-species. It really was a learning curve this time.

I also had to learn about the composition of the different jelly-like agar on which the organisms were grown. It reminded me of an advanced cookery book that contained recipes more complicated than any of those I had ever attempted at home. I needed to know how long the organisms took to grow, their normal habitat, what temperature they grew at, which of them liked oxygen and which did not. The odour of different organisms was also important; some had a very strong smell, like decaying meat and stale blood, and made you heave. The laboratory itself had a distinct and pungent odour, like rotten waste, but I soon didn't even notice it.

My new boss was the consultant microbiologist Professor Alistair Dudgeon, a close colleague of Dr Bill Marshall. He was in his sixties and dressed like a City gent in pinstriped trousers and jacket, with Brylcreemed black hair. He had been a pioneer in the research into the rubella vaccine for German measles. He was always very helpful, although I found him a bit austere at first, perhaps because he hadn't worked closely with nurses before, so wasn't sure how to treat me. I was the first infection control nurse at GOSH, so we both knew that it was a matter of learning on the job.

Everyone who worked in the lab wore white coats and I had to do likewise. On the plus side was the fact that everyone took their coffee, lunch and tea breaks, unlike on the wards where you were lucky to have a rest, let alone a cup of tea. The downside was the huge amount of work I had to do.

There was a strict hierarchical structure in the lab. Professor Dudgeon rarely spoke to anyone, but sent messages through his chief scientist, Mr Bill Hamilton, also in his sixties. He was knowledgeable and kind and I felt I could ask him anything, whereas I was more reserved with Professor Dudgeon. He would invite me into his office at coffee time, where a lot was discussed, and used to get annoyed if my bleep went off as it played havoc with his hearing aid. It bleeped frequently once people learnt about my new role and he would scowl at me angrily before continuing to talk.

I remember he once told me to take some swabs from a teddy bear in the play area, which grew MRSA. He soon recounted the story when lecturing, and would tell his audience 'We didn't have so much infection in the hospital until we appointed Susan Macqueen who found MRSA in the toys.' When I heard about this I laughed and realised that I would enjoy working with him.

Dr Bill Marshall was always ringing me about one problem or another, usually an infection on one of the wards. I knew he was determined to test me once again. He would march me round to the ward in question and wipe his fingers over the offending surfaces.

'Look at this dirt! Do something about it,' he would bark.

The cleaner on the cardiac unit was one of the doctor's biggest fans; she even used to clean his flat for him. She would listen to one of his tirades, nodding her head like one of those toys that hang from the back windows of cars, and would then ask everyone to move while she furiously mopped and wiped.

The cardiac unit was always causing us problems with infection. The surgeons would get very upset if a child developed an infection after having a valve or a patch implant, necessitating further heart surgery. I was learning how to differentiate between infections that were picked up in the hospital, as opposed to those acquired in the community – not always easy at that time, as many children did not have swabs taken on admission. My colleagues and I often debated how many of these children carried a bacteria germ called pseudomonas. Most of the children became carriers of the germ and were sometimes infected within twenty-four hours of admission, and were always washed in vinegar before surgery as this inhibits the germ's survival.

We were becoming increasingly concerned about

the way in which the tubing from ventilators was being decontaminated in a cubicle at the end of the ward. The tubing was washed over the sink in running tap water and then placed in Cidex, a strong-smelling disinfectant, which is no longer used because of its toxic nature. The tubes were soaked for at least an hour and then rinsed and hung up to dry on a line in the same cubicle. In an emergency they would often be used again before they had dried.

I remember one child, Harry, aged about fifteen, who had had a Gortex patch implanted to correct his cardiac defect. He was in the intensive care area and showing signs of infection and fever; various tests were also indicating a high white blood cell count.

Harry had been put on intravenous antibiotics, but two days later the labratory reported the organism was resistant to one of them. The antibiotics were changed, but by then several hours of treatment had been lost. Because Harry was showing signs of renal failure, he was put on renal dialysis. He was also on a ventilator and covered with tubes. Despite treatment, the signs of infection persisted and it was feared that the patch itself was contaminated. Antibiotics cannot penetrate artificial material, so the only alternative was to remove the patch, which was a very long and difficult procedure – a surgeon's nightmare.

Parents are always warned about the possible complications after surgery, including the risk of infection, but Harry's parents, Kerry and Alan, were devastated. They were staying in the parents' unit and took it in turns to be with him. Alan's boss had been good enough to give him paid time off, a relatively rare event, I think, especially then.

During this type of surgery there is an increased risk

of the patient dying, despite the skill of the surgeon. There is also the possibility of the new patch becoming infected, due to the previous patch being colonised by organisms sticking to the artificial material.

There was tension on the ward, as no one wants this to happen. As the parents were talked through the complex procedure, there were long silences while they processed the information.

'There's so much to take in,' Kerry said anxiously, as I went through it with them one more time.

Harry was taken to theatre and was there for several hours. One of the senior microbiologists had specified which antibiotics to use, the dose and the frequency of application. They had to be given on time, and twice during the procedure, as some of the dose would be lost, due to blood circulating round the heart machine that oxygenates the blood while the heart is stopped during surgery.

We were all keeping our fingers tightly crossed and Harry's poor parents walked up and down the corridors, endlessly pacing, while the operation was taking place.

'This is the worst moment of my life,' Kerry said, pale and teary.

Harry was brought back to the intensive care unit on a ventilator; he was on a number of IV infusions, had a urinary catheter in, and drains from his wounds were attached to underwater seal drainage to help expand his lungs and prevent them from collapsing. He needed two nurses to look after him as he was seriously ill. The next forty-eight hours would be critical.

I went round to the ward the following day, relieved to see that Harry was holding his own and Kerry and Alan were looking slightly less tense. It would be a few weeks yet before we could say that we were on top of the infection. Were the antibiotics just suppressing it or were they killing off the micro-organism?

Everyone knew that all the tubes Harry had inserted also posed a risk of infection, despite the best efforts of the staff. It was imperative that they were removed as soon as possible, but his life depended on them: a catch-22 situation. Harry was heavily sedated, so had no knowledge of his condition or his surroundings, unlike his parents who had to live with constant apprehension, loss of appetite and a feeling of lack of control.

Four days later, an attempt was made to reduce Harry's need for the ventilator. His sedation had also been reduced, but when his heart rate started to increase – a sign of distress – it was decided to delay taking him off the ventilator. Kerry looked on nervously when we decided to stop and try again the following day.

The next day, the same thing happened. This was a cause for concern. Had there been brain damage? Was Harry's diaphragm paralysed?

Over the next week things started to settle down and Harry was eventually taken off the ventilator after eight days. The chest drains had been taken out and his wounds were healing well. His white cell count was stabilising, along with his temperature.

Although he was still quite weak, Harry was now able to start talking to his parents again. The physiotherapist was doing a good job getting him out of bed and moving. He was transferred to a single cubicle and enjoyed watching TV and typical teenage shows like *Top of the Pops* and *Neighbours*. His blood counts were taken daily to keep an eye on progress and all was looking good.

A month after his operation Harry was allowed to go home, much to his own and his parents' relief. He would be followed up in outpatients regularly, until we were sure his infection had been eradicated, and there was no residual effect on his kidneys. Another miracle had occurred.

During this time, we investigated the possible source of Harry's infection. The suspected cause was the ventilator equipment, in which case it would prove to be a hospital-acquired infection. The cubicle, where the respiratory equipment was cleaned, was in a worse state than anyone had imagined; old plaster was sticking to the tubes after 'cleaning' and things were not being done correctly. The system had fallen down completely, but no one was taking direct responsibilty. The ventilator technician had been doing his best, but admitted to being overwhelmed by his workload. Swabs were taken from the equipment both inside and outside the decontamination room, and tests indicated that all had grown the same organism. This was the scientific proof we needed that the system had to change.

An outbreak action meeting took place, attended by senior medical staff, nurses, administrators and managers of relevant units, including decontamination. We explained what had happened, backed up by statistics, and presented a plan of action. Surgery should be postponed in the case of children needing ventilators; the equipment should be decontaminated in washing machines in another hospital unit; and more ventilator tubing must be purchased. It was proposed that this regime should start as soon as possible. In the interim period, I had done some research into the type of washing machines I would need in the hospital, and found they were made in Germany.

The hospital had always been supportive of infection control, and they took action. We made sure that the chief executive was kept informed of the details. While costly to implement, the new system was long overdue. It took a few months to introduce the changes, but we eventually did complete them. Over time, the organism causing the problem was greatly reduced and fewer children were found to be colonised.

It had been a success: my new journey had started.

I headed back to my office ready to fight the next round of infections, knowing that I would always be looking out for the children – first and always.

# Epilogue

*London, 27 July 2012*

The logo of a child's round face, with a single tear falling from its eye, magically lights up my living room in a bright blue and white glow. I feel a swell of pride and surprise bubble up inside me, like fizzy water. Of the many children's hospitals across the country, the director, Danny Boyle, has chosen Great Ormond Street Hospital as the one to celebrate in the opening ceremony of the London Olympics.

Hundreds of children bounce on luminous beds; doctors and nurses perform a joyful jive, and a handful of real-life patients and staff wave to the cheering audience, to the hypnotic sound of Mike Oldfield's famous 'Tubular Bells'. Tonight is all about inspiring the next generation and children are the making of the nation.

As the sequence featuring the NHS and Great Ormond Street Hospital unfolds, I am thrilled, but most of all intrigued as to how something as big as this has been kept secret. But I shouldn't have wondered for a second how they managed it. Many children of high-profile parents, stars, diplomats and members of the royal family are treated at the hospital, and even in cases where something exceedingly unusual has taken place, and is reported in the press, you never know the details – even if you are only a few metres away on another ward. The hospital is renowned for maintaining people's privacy and confidentiality, something I have always admired and respected.

During my years in infection control, I learnt a great deal. I was now in a stronger position to help prevent hospital-acquired infections in children. I learnt how to recognise outbreaks and put preventive measures in place, and to influence my colleagues, at least some-times, to adopt practices which were well known but not always followed, such as hand hygiene. I learnt more about management and leadership and networked furi-ously to acquire more knowledge. I gained a reputation for getting things done and would often be called upon to deal with blocked drains and other unpleasant problems.

As well as attending regional and national meetings, I was invited to join various Department of Health com-mittees, which helped me to understand the way gov-ernment worked. GOSH were very supportive and I was allowed time off to pursue these activities. Although my heart is still with the children, I have found that the only way to influence progress and improve standards of care is by going to the top. You can never do this on your own, but only by persuading people with influence to make a difference. You have to be focused, profes-sional, tenacious and patient. I like to think I have some of these traits.

I was a Royal College of Nursing activist (or RCN stew-ard, as they were known then) for thirty-eight years. I received training for this role in negotiation, the law at work, health and safety, recruitment and retention, employment relations and policy writing. Working in the lab and not on the ward gave me more flexible time for my studies.

Due to my drug-error incident many years before, I also gradually became interested in supporting nurses during difficult times: nurses who found themselves in front of their managers or suspended from work because of drug errors, poor performance, clinical and decision-making errors, stress, and mental health issues such as depression. On rare occassions, I have been involved in supporting nurses through abuse with their partners, when accused of stealing drugs or when blamed for child abuse themselves. I learnt so much about the pressures which nurses and others are under when performing health care, and also about professional accountability, that seemed paramount to me. It is important that a nurse is dealt with in an empathetic, fair manner. Sometimes I didn't think this was the case and I usually said so. Sometimes the nurse was at fault and I always took the opportunity to make the point that, generally, no nurse makes a mistake intentionally. Sometimes it is the process that is wrong and that needs to be corrected.

I finally left GOSH in 2010, after trying to retire three times, and I still work for the hospital in an advisory capacity. I travel to many countries across the globe to share experiences with those in nursing, medicine and allied professions such as speech therapy, dietetics, pharmacy and occupational therapy. We always say that 'good teamwork' is the answer to good care.

In the early 1990s, I bought a flat in the same block as John's, in Tufnell Park, north London. We continued to spend time together and gradually fell properly in love.

I enjoyed his warmth, easy humour and intelligent conversation – and still do. In 1993, I went with a friend to Hatton Garden where I chose an engagement ring and announced to John that he needed to buy it for me. I dragged him along to see it, even though he had a cold at the time. Again he didn't put up a fight. It wasn't until six years later, in 1999, that we were finally married in a lovely, intimate ceremony for our friends and family. It was a wonderful day and even though the relationship was a slow-burning one, I know John is my soul mate.

John and I are just two of the millions of people watching the opening ceremony of the Olympics unfold and the scene in our front room is similar, I imagine, to many all over the country. After dinner we sit side by side on the sofa with mugs of coffee and argue over who is in control of the remote. John usually wins but tonight we are in agreement. Outside, the street which is normally humming with the noise of people and traffic seems eerily quiet and I imagine everyone is glued to their television screens. Like many, I had found the constant negative press which had surrounded the event somewhat frustrating, especially the hysteria over the likelihood of the London transport system crumbling and public services threatening to go on strike for the period of the Games. Why were people asking for more money when they were just doing their jobs? It brought to mind the London bombings on 7 July 2005, when all NHS workers and other public services excelled themselves in striving to save lives. At GOSH, the staff canteen had been turned into a casualty department for people caught in the bombing at Russell Square. The hospital staff even went to the tube station to help injured people; some arrived before the emergency services, putting themselves in great danger. I know it was different, a crisis, an emergency, but no one asked for extra money or time off; we were all just doing our jobs.

I think about the day I first walked through the hospital doors, excited and nervous about the next chapter in my nursing career. By that point I knew children's nursing was for me and I wanted to learn as much as I could about it. As a kaleidoscope of images runs through my head, I think about the different experiences I have had over the years, the gummy-wide smiles of the children, the fear masked quickly by spikes of adrenalin, the wonderful successes greeted by whoops of delight from families; and also about the tragic failures, despite the best efforts of science and human endeavour.

Progress in medicine over the last forty years has been almost unbelievable, but the battle against disease and infection is relentless. The images before me on my screen show the happy, caring faces of the Mary Poppins of nursing, but my mind keeps wandering to lonely night shifts, the smell of carbolic, the desperate cries of parents and the dulcet sounds of a sleeping ward, and wondering what the next day will bring, but above all, the dedication and commitment of the medical staff.

The techniques and the science have improved, but the importance of the nursing staff can never be overstated. It is the determination and commitment of these foot soldiers in the never-ending war against illness and infection, who provide the shoulder to cry on, the teddy to play with, the midnight jam sandwich and the million and one things in between.

Unlike many of our friends and neighbours, John and I had decided to stay put in our Highgate home for the duration of the Olympics. I had confidence in our national reputation for always putting on a good show and as I sit watching the weird, wonderful and wacky celebration, I know my gut feeling was right all along.

As we sit, captivated, my phone beeps melodiously as texts arrive from former GOSH colleagues who are equally astonished that the hospital is playing such a prominent role. A giant, ghostly Lord Voldemort from the Harry Potter books looms over the performers, a massive paper baby fills my screen as an army of twinkling Mary Poppins float across the sky and J. K. Rowling reads from J. M. Barrie's classic *Peter Pan*. In the figure of Peter Pan, GOSH found its perfect patron – thanks to the author's generosity, it will be connected for ever with the boy who never grew up. The hospital sees many, many children who get better and leave, giggling and skipping out through the doors with their futures ahead of them and the renewed chance to grow up. Sadly, some children are destined to stay young for ever. But regardless of this, unlike adults, the patients are rarely sad or sorry for themselves. The picture on my screen captures the energy and vibrancy of childhood, where small things really matter, like laughter and fun.

The young patients are the very heartbeat, voice and soul of the place. The hospital's motto, 'The child first and always', as well as being a code of practice, is a celebration of childhood and everything it stands for. What a wonderful snapshot of GOSH.

For competitions, author interviews,
pre-publication extracts,
news and events,
sign up to the monthly

# Orion Books Newsletter

at
www.orionbooks.co.uk

Follow us on twitter @orionbooks